Sincerely, Brother Griff

Volume 2

ANOTHER BOOK OF INSPIRATION & HOPE

GIL BURNETT GRIFFIN

Print ISBN: 978-1-66785-150-1

Printed in the United States of America

TABLE OF CONTENTS

Sincerely, Brother Griff

Volume 2

INTRODUCTION

———— ～ ————

We live in an ever changing world. Truth, compassion, morality and common sense are all becoming rare commodities. Many people are devoid of any type of spiritual connection to our Lord & Savior Jesus Christ. Many of the signs of the times that we now see unfolding all around us were foretold in scriptures centuries ago. The manifestation of these signs can be witnessed everywhere you look!

"<u>Sincerely, Brother Griff Volume 2</u>" is my second attempt to introduce Christianity to our brothers and sisters who are incarcerated. Comprised of fifteen individual letters, each letter offers a message and an invitation to accept Jesus Christ into your life. My goal is to help those individuals who feel helpless, hopeless and rejected, to learn that Papa Jesus is knocking at the doors of their hearts and awaiting the opportunity to come into their lives. Since the publication of my first book, I have witnessed many people accept Jesus Christ as their personal Lord and Savior. I have also witnessed blatant rejection of Him no matter how much evidence of His existence was presented. Sad yet true!

No matter if you are incarcerated or not, no matter what your station in life is, **Jesus Lives** and **Jesus Saves!** In the following pages you will be given biblical, spiritual and inspirational advice on how to attain a closer walk with The Lord. The messages contained within, are valuable, relevant and useful for a myriad of Christian based outreach programs. I therefore dedicate this book to my Lord and Savior Jesus Christ who deserves all the praise and all the glory. Please open your mind, open your heart and learn exactly what Papa Jesus can do for you, if you just give Him a chance!

CHAPTER ONE

———— ≈ ————

Our Greatest Hope

August 14th, 2020

Dear Friend,

Greetings in the name of our Lord and Savior Jesus Christ! It is my sincerest wish that this letter will find you doing as well as possible despite your surroundings. No matter where you are, in your jail cell, in the hole, on the main yard or in the hospital/infirmary, **Jesus Loves You!** Our Lord is omnipresent which means that He is everywhere at the same time. He is omnipotent, meaning that He is all powerful. Lastly, He is omniscient, meaning that He is all knowing. Having created each one of us, He knows us better than we know ourselves. These three characteristics makes Him **Our Greatest Source Of Hope In A Hopeless World!**

Let's take a look at the word hope. Hope is something that leads an individual to believe that there is still a chance that things can change for the better. It implies that the present situation, or set of circumstances, has room for improvement. Being in a government run penal facility, you the reader, are inevitably forced to agree with me that things could be better for you. No matter what your crime was, no matter how long your sentence is, things can only get better. Which brings us back to the word hope. Hope, is something those on the inside and those on the outside, always have regarding our basic state of affairs!

So now that we've defined hope, let's look at the word hopeless. At some point in time, we have all felt as if a particular situation, or set of circumstances, was hopeless. There was no foreseeable way out, there was no positive outcome visible anywhere on the horizon. Hope seemed like a distant memory or something applicable to everyone other than yourself. But not you. Hopeless, was the only word that you could use to describe your plight. Everyone who has ever lived, with the exception of Jesus Christ, can agree that they viewed their condition as hopeless at some point in time!

In Greek mythology, the story of Pandora speaks of this. Pandora was given a box and was told to guard it with her life, but never open it. One simple request, one simple rule. Could she abide by it? No, for when she opened the box, every bad/evil thing that now plagues our world escaped from the box. Every horrible thing that you can imagine, Pandora released into the world. However, despite curiosity getting the best of her, and, personally being the cause of all negative trauma that the world now endures, only one thing was left in the box. Do you know what it was? **Hope!**

Adam and Eve were given a solitary charge just like Pandora. They were placed in the Garden Of Eden and lived in a lush paradise. In order to eat, all they had to do was walk up to a fruit tree and eat whatever they desired. They could walk up to a grape vine or a berry bush and feast on the bounty of the garden. God The Father gave them one proviso, never eat of the fruit of the tree of knowledge of good and evil. For if they did, they would surely die. Guess what they did? They broke the one and only rule that they were given. And look at us now. We now reap the benefits of original sin, that original sin of disobedience to Almighty God The Father!

Which brings us back again to hope. Pandora had the hope that some day, some way and some how, things would possibly get better. Adam and Eve, even though they were blessed with the rare opportunity to walk and talk with and see Almighty God The Father, having fallen from grace, still believed that there was hope. That magical four letter word upon which very few other words carry more weight. Hope, that precious miracle that you pray will happen when you face the most dire of circumstances. What Princess Leia told Obi-Wan Kenobi when she left that infamous message with R2D2 in the movie Star Wars; "Help me Obi-Wan Kenobi, you're my only hope!" Hope, that precious commodity that we place all of our dreams and aspirations in!

Jesus Christ is the antidote to hopelessness and He is the embodiment of hope. When God The Father saw that man had chosen to disobey Him, He still had so much love and compassion for mankind that He vowed to send His only begotten Son to save the world. He didn't have to, but that shows just how much God loves us. Yes, God was angry with man. Yes, God had every right to be upset with the being that He created on the sixth day in His own image. Yes, Almighty God punished man for original sin and yes, man was lucky that he wasn't punished more severely. However, His anger subsided and He implemented **The Plan Of Salvation** so that a sinful and lost mankind could have a second chance at what Adam and Eve took for granted. That single act of disobedience opened up a plethora of woes to mankind that we are still feeling the effect of today!

Hopelessness runs rampant in this "Me First" society of self centered sinners. Mankind has replaced the love of Almighty God with the love of the almighty dollar. Smart phones, social media and technology get more attention than faith, prayer and places of worship. Satan has continuously attempted to divert the attention of mankind from Jesus Christ to the latest gadget and gizmo of the day. He deceived Eve, and in like manner, attempts to deceive mankind as a whole with his diversionary tactics and parlor tricks.

But do not be deceived, Jesus Christ died on the cross to save a lost and sinful mankind. That paradise that Adam and Eve lost so long ago is now available to anyone who is willing to repent of their sinful ways and accept Jesus Christ as their personal Lord and Savior. John chapter 11 verses 25 & 26 states;

25. Jesus said unto her, "I am the resurrection, and the life: he that believeth in me, though he were dead, yet shall he live."

26. "And whosoever liveth and believeth in me shall never die. Believeth thou this?"

Jesus is hope for the hopeless, He is the way for the wayward and He is the only direction for the lost. Jesus can work unbelievable miracles for you if you would just open up the door of your heart and let Him in. He is the best thing to be addicted to because He will always watch over you and deliver you from evil. He has done this for billions of people. What makes you think that He cannot do this for you? In the first paragraph I told you that he is omnipotent. He has the power to do as He pleases. If you come to Him with a sincere desire to change your life for the better and depart from your sinful ways, He will use His power to work unprecedented miracles in your life. Hope is what He is. The greatest hope that mankind will ever have is in His Holy Name, Jesus Christ. Help to the helpless and hope for the hopeless. Ask Him to come into your life and let Him be the answer to your hopelessness. May Almighty God Bless You And Direct Your Path!

Sincerely,

Brother Griff

Chapter Two

--- ∾ ---

Put On The Whole Armor Of Christ

October 1st, 2020

Dear Friend,

I greet you in the name of Our Lord and Savior Jesus Christ! I am writing this letter to you on the first day of the beginning of the fourth quarter of the year 2020. It is October 1st in what has turned out to be one of the most remarkable years in human history. In this year we have seen the stock market reach historic highs and subsequently drop to record setting lows. We've seen the Covid-19 pandemic wipe out over 200,000 U.S.

Citizens and infect millions worldwide. Racial unrest has ravaged our nation on levels that have greatly surpassed The 1960's, and, police brutality worldwide has been highlighted like never before. Unemployment has swept our country now worse than during the great depression and our towns, cities and states cannot agree on how to re-open their economies after being shut down for months. Large gatherings have been eliminated and on top of it all, this is an election year. 2020 has indeed been a year of astronomical changes but despite all this, Jesus Christ is still sitting on the throne of Heaven and He is still, without a shadow of a doubt, in control!

It is very easy to look at what is going on in the world and come to the conclusion that things are spiraling out of control. Watching the nightly news broadcasts can truly blow your mind with the ever increasing and never ending chaos that is enveloping our planet. The Holy Bible has predicted these happenings and has foretold of things to come which will be far worse than what we are witnessing today. Those who do not have a relationship with Jesus Christ can look at these events and think that there is no hope. They can feel the anxiety of these events and run to a liquor store or a cannabis dispensary to attempt to ease the effects of this worldwide trauma. However, sedating yourself is not the answer. When your buzz is gone, when the hangover dissipates, guess what? The trauma is still there and all you've done is postpone dealing with the inevitable. Running from a situation or a set of circumstances is never the answer. Life must be confronted head on. Establishing, building and maintaining a relationship with Our Lord and Savior Jesus Christ is the only protection we have against the chaos that Satan is perpetuating around the world. Establishing, building and maintaining a relationship with Jesus will enable you to put on the whole armor of Christ so that you will have the physical, mental and spiritual tools needed to thrive in an otherwise chaotic and maniacal world.

Jesus offers us life like we've never known it. He offers us truth and light. He is the giver of all good things and most of all, He is our Creator, our Redeemer and our Sustainer. Jesus watches over and protects His own. Now this is not to say that if you give your life to Jesus, nothing bad will ever happen to you. All things that happen to any person on the planet have to go by Him first and foremost. If Jesus doesn't want something to happen to you, it won't. You must remember that adversity is God's way of drawing us closer to Him. Adversity is our chance to grow in our faith and in our spiritual strength. A Christian realizes this whereas a non-believer doesn't!

The establishment of a relationship with Jesus consists of repenting of your sins, getting baptized and reading God's word. If you are able to join a Bible based Church that is even better. Learning how to pray is vital in this phase because prayer is how we can reach out to God and let Him know that we are sorry for our sinful ways. This is the phase where you call on God for His love, guidance and mercy. During The Establishment Phase, you are reaching out to God and letting Him know that you are willing to leave your sinful past in order to make Jesus a part of your present and future!

The Building Phase of a relationship with Jesus Christ consists of Bible study and getting a better understanding of exactly who God is. Prayer is a vital part of this phase because The Lord wants us to have constant communication with Him through the power of prayer. Jesus wants to hear from you and wants to know what's in your heart. Through prayer and Bible study your knowledge of Him will increase. The Bible is full of stories of people who have been in situations and circumstances greater than or equal to yours. These stories can help you to realize how you fit into the overall Christian picture!

The Maintenance Phase consists of getting involved with a Bible based Church and participating in the activities therein. You might have a gift for singing or would like to become a Deacon or even an Associate Minister. The possibilities are endless. Prayer and Bible study increase with greater exposure to the Christian community. With God, all things are possible and with increased exposure to the Christian community, you will see how the chaos of the world we now live in was predicted long ago. When you put on the whole armor of Jesus Christ, you will see that the only thing worth fearing in this world is displeasing Our Lord and Savior!

Establish, build and maintain. These are the three essential components of having a relationship with Our Lord and Savior Jesus Christ. As you can see, prayer is essential in each and every phase. It is the most vital component in communication with Jesus. Putting on the whole armor of Christ means that you have made the conscious decision to follow Him and turn from a life of sin. Does this mean that you will never sin again? Absolutely not, however, being a baptized believer in Jesus Christ means that all of your sins, past, present and future, were nailed to that old rugged cross when He died on Calvary. Your debt of sin was paid for before you were even born. Acknowledgment of Jesus Christ as Lord of all, places you on a collision course with everlasting life in His Kingdom. Putting on the whole armor of Christ will enable you to repel the onslaughts that we Christians deal with from a satanic foe. The imps and emissaries of the Devil are always attempting to derail our relationship with our Heavenly Father. The whole armor of Christ readies you for the battles we must face when it comes to temptation and our faith is always being tested by a ruthless and relentless adversary. It enables you to speak plainly and confidently about the one who turned your life around and gave you a chance when your luck had run out. Also, it allows you to win souls for Christ by setting an example that others would like to follow, thereby, making you a role model for believers and non-believers alike. Therefore, I implore you, to put on the whole armor of Christ. Without it, we are destined for defeat and failure!

Put On The Whole Armor Of Christ! Jesus is the best person to have as a friend, advocate and Savior. People will let you down, Jesus won't. He will provide for you, care for you, help you, comfort you and sustain you. He'll be everything that people should be, but aren't. **Put On The Whole Armor Of Christ!** He will make a way when there is no way. He is The Creator of all that we know and He is more than able to create a better way of life for you. He knows what you want and furthermore knows what you need, and, He ultimately knows you better than you know yourself. Give Him your trust, give Him your faith and give Him your life, subsequently, He will give you confidence in your eternal destination and happiness like you've never known before. **Put On The Whole Armor Of Christ!**

Ephesians chapter 6 verse 11 says it like this;

"Put on the whole armor of God, that ye may be able to stand against the wiles of the devil."

Put On The Whole Armor Of Christ! The rewards will be unimaginable. Things are getting worse day by day and the things that we have witnessed in 2020 are amazing in comparison to what we witnessed in 2019. Just think what we will have witnessed by this time next year if we are allowed to still be here. **Put On The Whole Armor Of Christ!** Eternity has no end, however, your time to procrastinate is definitely limited. Therefore, make the wise decision. The brief years that you will live in time are nothing compared to the countless eons you will spend in eternity. Papa Jesus guarantees eternal life for the believer. Satan guarantees false promises and eternal damnation. What would you rather have and which guarantee works the best for you? Please take the time to think about that carefully my friend. Thank you for your time and God bless you!

Sincerely,

Brother Griff

CHAPTER THREE

·≈·

Evaluation & Adjustments

October 30th, 2020

Dear Friend,

I hope that this letter finds you doing well. As this year rapidly comes to a close I am truly amazed at what I have witnessed in person and on the news. Although this year has been a year unlike any that I've ever seen, I can't help but think of how different things are now as opposed to how they were at this point in time last year. Last year at this time, we were preparing for Halloween. Last minute searches for just the right costume for my wife and daughter, in addition to, planning our itinerary for the night. Due to the global pandemic, this year has forced many people to rethink and reinvent exactly how they will celebrate this holiday and remain safe at the same time. This has also forced many around the world to evaluate and adjust their plans accordingly.

Evaluation and adjustments are very important in many various aspects of our lives. On a scholastic level, evaluation and adjustments are vital in determining the growth of a student. Testing, measures how well students have retained their comprehension of the course curriculum and allows teachers to decide if the progress shown deserves promotion to the next grade or not. In sports, evaluation and adjustments have to be executed slowly or on a lightning fast level dependent upon the sport itself. For example, the speed in which you evaluate and adjust are much slower in a football game as compared to a boxing match. Whereas both sports have time outs, the amount of time outs is limited in football yet unlimited in boxing. However, the speed in which you evaluate and adjust in boxing is much faster because failure to do so can end up with you getting knocked out. Quarterbacks, Linebackers and Safeties can call an audible in a football game to change the play when the teams line up, and failure to do so can result in disaster. However, football players have a lot more time to execute an adjustment than a boxer does!

Financially, people have to look at their assets and adjust how they allocate their funds. The stock market, 401k and investment plans, have all been used to help people acquire and manage their wealth. Failure to evaluate their situation and make the necessary adjustments, can result in financial ruin. The same is true with careers. When kids turn into teenagers, they see something that they like and their parents tell them that they need to get a summer job and work toward making that purchase. Summer jobs are an excellent way to enter the work force, however, many people do not want to make a career out of working at a car wash or scooping ice cream at an ice cream parlor. Therefore, evaluation and adjustments need to be made in order to attain career oriented employment and not just a summer job.

Relationships can be one of the most vital examples of evaluation and adjustments. At some point, we all have been in a relationship where we have been forced to evaluate the relationship itself and determine whether or not the relationship is working out for the best. Sometimes, after much evaluation and assessment, we have made the decision to stick with someone and work things out. Alternately, we have also made the decision to depart from someone. All of these examples illustrate just how important evaluation and adjustments can be in this life. However, the most important aspect of this can be seen when it comes to our eternal souls!

Take a good look at where you stand with God right now. If you were to stand in front of Him today, would there be a smile on His face as He looked upon you, or a frown? Many people do not think about their standing with God which is the biggest and most consequential mistake a person could ever make. If you were to say that you thought that God would be smiling at you when He saw you, then I assume that you have confessed your sins to Him and have accepted Jesus Christ as your personal Lord and Savior. But what if He was frowning when He looked upon you?

If you were to say that you think that God would be frowning when He saw you, then ask yourself why? Why would my creator be frowning at me as He looked upon me? Bam! Time for evaluation! Look at what you have or have not been doing. Look at who you have or have not been associating with. Look at how much you have or have not been praying. Look at how often you have or have not attended Church or any type of Bible study. Look at how much you have or have not read your Bible. Do you even own a Bible? Evaluate yourself using this criteria. Do you believe in God? Do you believe that Jesus Christ is His Son and that He was born of The Virgin Mary and died for our sins? Do you believe that He rose on the third day and is now seated on the right hand side of God The Father? Do you believe that He will return and will establish His Kingdom on Earth? Do you want to be a part of His Eternal Kingdom?

If your answer is yes, then now is the time for some adjustments. If your answer to the last six questions was no, guess what? There is still hope for you. In the early 1990's, a common catch phrase on the street was, "Ya better check yourself, before you wreck yourself." Back in the first century, the apostle Paul in writing letters to the church at Corinth essentially stated the same thing. First Corinthians chapter 11 verses 31 and 32 says this:

31. For if we would judge ourselves, we should not be judged.

32. But when we are judged, we are chastened of the Lord, that we should not be condemned with the world.

God wants us to live in harmony with Him. If your lifestyle has been in compliance with God's Word, evaluate your relationship with Him so that you can become even closer to Him. If your lifestyle has been in opposition to God's Word, you still have time to self evaluate and make the necessary adjustments in order to get into a harmonious relationship with The Lord. He wants us to judge ourselves so that when we are judged by Him, we will escape condemnation by becoming chastened of The Lord. That can only be accomplished by self evaluation and making the necessary adjustments so that your lifestyle is pleasing to Almighty God!

Jesus loves you and is waiting for you to invite Him into your heart. He wants you to enjoy eternal happiness as opposed to eternal damnation. The price of admission is simple. Confess and repent of your sins and invite Jesus Christ to become your personal Lord and Savior. Belief in Him grants you eternal life because you have agreed to turn from a life of sin. Get baptized and adjust your thought process. Pick up a Bible and read it from cover to cover. When you have finished, read it again and again. Learn the word of God. Reject Satan and all of his empty promises. Refocus your thoughts from things of this world to things eternal. Let Papa Jesus be the role model for your future. He will change your life in ways that you never thought were possible!

You have a golden opportunity to make the most important evaluation and adjustments in your life right now. Today is the day when things can begin to change for **you** for the better. Don't procrastinate, don't ruin a beautiful opportunity to join a winning team. Hell is no place desirable and once there inescapable. Hell has one way in and no way out. Once there, we can stick a fork in **you**, because **you, will be done.** No one can help **you** and nothing can save **you**. Please don't let that be your fate! Fate is defined as: "The development of events beyond a person's control, regarded as determined by a supernatural power." Papa Jesus is that supernatural power and **you** have the ability to control your activities and actions regarding your fate. Please evaluate and adjust your life now so that the joy of eternal life can be yours. Please evaluate and re-evaluate your life and make the necessary adjustments. Look at how many times the word **you** was emphasized in this paragraph. **You** have the ability to redirect your eternal destination. Look at what **you** are doing and at what **you** have been doing. Can **you** honestly say that The Lord is pleased with your behavior? Whether **you** go to Heaven or go to Hell, **you**, will be the blame! Accept the blame for making the right decision. Don't waste this opportunity my friend, Heaven awaits!

Sincerely,

Brother Griff

CHAPTER FOUR

Trajectory

December 2nd, 2020

Dear Friend,

I am honored to be able to greet you again in the name of our Lord and Savior Jesus Christ. Today, I would like to talk to you about trajectory. Trajectory is defined as the path followed by a projectile flying or an object moving under the action of given forces. There are certain other words that correspond with the word trajectory. Here are a few of them: course, route, path, track, line, orbit, flight path, direction, bearing, way and approach. In my last letter I focused on evaluation and adjustments. I therefore would like to draw your attention to the word trajectory.

Let's start off with the simplest of questions, where are you headed? Currently, you are incarcerated. That defines where you presently are at this point in time. But where are you headed? That question can be answered by looking at your trajectory. Go back to the first paragraph and look at the definition again. Trajectory is defined as the path followed by a projectile flying or an object moving under the action of given forces. We, as human beings, completely fall under both categories of this definition. We all were metaphorically shot out of a cannon, that cannon being our mother's womb, and placed into this world. Our world is the third planet in orbit around our sun. Our planet is not stationary, it rotates on its axis. That rotation gives us our days and our nights. At the same time, our planet orbits the sun on a path that takes 365 to 366 days to complete. Thereby creating our years. We are therefore flying around the sun and moving under the action of given forces. But where are you headed?

In my last letter I asked you to take a good look at where you are now actually, physically, metaphorically and spiritually. I asked you to evaluate your spiritual situation and determine if you feel that you are on course for your desired eternal destination. Have you given that proposition any thought since then? Have you taken a good look at your present set of surroundings and thanked Almighty God that you are there and not someplace worse? Have you seriously started to think about where you want to stay on an eternal basis? Will you have a beautiful mansion on Hallelujah Avenue or will your eternal destination be somewhat warmer? If you believe that you are on course for that preferred Heavenly destination, then no adjustments are necessary, but if not, then your trajectory is off course. Bringing us back to that magical question, where are you headed?

I know that currently, you are not where you **want** to be and that you are where you **have** to be. Thankfully, that will not always be the case. Either you will be released from prison or you will die in prison. In each scenario, you will be going somewhere else. Right now, I beg of you to take time to seriously think about that. I know that the status quo seems to stay stuck on, **the here and now**, a lot longer than we'd all like. In prison, I'm told, that time really does stand still. No matter how fast or how slow it takes, change is definitely coming. Will you be prepared for that change when it eventually gets here or not? If you were to die in your current spiritual state, would you be happy when you arrived on the other side or horrified? Would Papa Jesus be awaiting you with open arms or Satan? These questions are definitely things that make you go hmm!

Think back to the act, or series of actions, that got you incarcerated. Somehow and someway a crime was committed. I want you to stop right there and think of how blessed you are right now. Now I bet you are asking yourself, "How can I be blessed and I'm locked up here in prison?" Well, think back to the commission of that crime and how everything went down. Honestly, it didn't have to have happened that way. Actually, you could have died. Now, if you did die right then, where do you think that you would be right now? Before you answer that question, remember, you died in the act of committing a crime. Almighty God had mercy on you. You might not have seen it then and you might not see it now, but just ponder this for a moment. Wouldn't you rather be alive and in prison with a second chance to get yourself right with The Lord, or, would you rather be roasting in Hell right now with no chance of receiving Salvation and Mercy?

I know that prison is no church picnic nor was it meant to be. However, you now have the fortunate opportunity to look at your trajectory, evaluate your path and make the necessary adjustments to your course, so that your eternal destination will be one that you will enjoy. A lot of people have died in the commission of crimes, where do you think that they are right now? Don't you think that they would gladly trade places with you if they could? Papa Jesus loves you so much, that instead of letting you die foolishly, He gave you a second chance at developing a relationship with Him. You have the amazing opportunity to turn away from sin and ask Papa Jesus to forgive you for your past and activate your future with Him as the centerpiece of your life. You have the power to turn to your Creator, your Redeemer and your Sustainer, and repent. Repentance leads to Mercy and Mercy is the gateway to Salvation. Papa Jesus doesn't wish fire and brimstone on anyone. That is a fate which is completely avoidable, however, we share this world with a lot of individuals who believe that they know it all. They think that God, Satan, Heaven, Hell, Angels and Demons, are just the stuff of legends, myths and fairy tales. Unbelievers make up the majority of every crowd that you are in. **Don't join the crowd!**

Ask The Lord to come into your heart and divorce you from your sinful past. Ask Him to send The Holy Spirit to wash away your sins and flush out the evil that dwells in your heart and mind. Our God is loving, strong, powerful, eternal and everlasting. He is a friend to the friendless and He is hope to the hopeless. He is a lifeline to those who are drowning in sin and He is the rock that you can build your relationship with Him on. He is the Father of Faith and the Master of Mercy. He will lead you through your troubled times and carry you when your strength runs out. He is someone who will never know defeat and He is always there when you need Him. There is nothing that He cannot accomplish and there is no problem that He cannot solve. He can help you out of any predicament that you may find yourself in and He will always defy the odds. Give Him your heart and watch the results. Give Him your faith and your trust and He will deliver you to that eternal destination that will make you shout, "Blessed Assurance, Jesus Is Mine!" My friend, check your trajectory and make sure that your course is aimed directly at Jesus. Heaven is the only eternal destination that you want to call your home. That is the only trajectory worth your while! May Almighty God continue to bless your trajectory and guide your path!

Sincerely,

Brother Griff

CHAPTER FIVE

~

Happy New Year!

January 7th, 2021

Dear Friend,

I greet you in the name of Our Lord and Savior Jesus Christ. Happy New Year! Yesterday, the U.S. Capital building was stormed by supporters of President Donald Trump and 5 people were killed. These individuals felt justified in their rampage because of exactly who they put their faith in. They placed their faith and allegiance in a man who has consistently lied to them and ultimately spurred them onto violent behavior. I watched how a leader and his followers took the law into their own hands and attempted to thwart our democracy by storming the U.S. Capital, endeavoring to overturn the results of a fair and legitimate election. I therefore was reminded of what God The Father said in the book of Exodus to the children of Israel. In Exodus chapter 23 verses 1 and 2 it reads as follows:

1. Thou shalt not raise a false report, put not thine hand with the wicked to be an unrighteous witness.

2. Thou shalt not follow a multitude to do evil: neither shalt thou speak in a cause to decline after many wrest judgment.

Faith is a beautiful thing. Faith is the foundation for relationships. When faith is lost, the relationship falters and ultimately fails. When the object of faith is rock solid, true and secure, faith blossoms. When the object of faith is deceitful, misguided and flawed, faith becomes cult-like, erroneous and destined for failure. In other words, if you put your faith in Jesus Christ you are destined for eternal blessings. Faith in anything or anyone else, is doomed and destined for destruction and eternal damnation. Confidence in flesh is misplaced yet confidence in Jesus Christ will always bear great dividends!

Second Peter chapter 2 verse 10 speaks of this and it reads as follows;

"But chiefly them that walk after the flesh in the lust of uncleanness, and despise government. Presumptuous are they, self-willed, they are not afraid to speak evil of dignities."

That one little verse encapsulates and also speaks volumes in regards to the collective mindset of this particular group of individuals. The still and video images of these people, and what they did, completely brings this verse to life. The following of a false teacher or of a false prophet will undoubtedly lead to ruin. Had Jesus chosen to return at that point in time, it is safe to say that none of these individuals would have inherited the Kingdom Of Heaven. Their faith was misplaced and their hearts were set on doing evil and committing sin. This is just another illustration of how relevant The Holy Bible is today, even though it was written centuries ago!

The news media spent most of the night reporting on this historic event and will continue to do so for quite some time. This event will go down in American history as an event which will be remembered as a very tragic and dark day for our country. In the same light as the Kennedy and Lincoln assassinations, the attack at Pearl Harbor, the assassinations of Medgar Evers, Malcolm X and Martin Luther King Jr., and the destruction of the World Trade Center on September 11th, 2001. I was shocked myself to actually witness these events unfolding on my television, however, I was not surprised. Having lived through The 1960's and witnessing The Anti-Vietnam War Protests, The Black Panther Movement and The Civil Rights Movement. I actually thought that this type of thing would have taken place in The 1970's since The 1960's got this snowball started rolling downhill. I personally believe that we are living in the days of prophecy being fulfilled and I also believe that the advent of Covid-19 has placed a line in the sand between the good old days and the last days of time!

Covid-19 has ushered in the new era of civilization. It brought about social distancing, the wearing of face masks, Zoom meetings, working from home and an overall change in the way we do things worldwide. Conducting business is different, education is different, banking is different, dining, relaxing, worshiping, exercising, socializing and shopping are all completely different now than the way they were prior to this worldwide pandemic known as Covid-19!

The times have changed and yet they are a changing. Things aren't the way they used to be and they aren't as bad as they are going to get. Belief in Jesus Christ is the only protection available to us in these turbulent satanic times. **"Jesus is the way, the truth and the life. No man cometh unto The Father but by Him."** Those who don't believe can become easily terrified by the events that are unraveling all around us. Political unrest, wars, rumors of wars, unemployment, chaos, pestilences, famines, natural disasters, global warming, crime, poverty and an overall lack of compassion can be seen wherever you are located on the globe. And it's getting worse. People who don't know The Lord are flocking to marijuana dispensaries, liquor stores, pharmacies and drug dealers, looking for a way to escape the anxiety associated with living in the world of today. I'm here to tell you that sedatives are not the answer. **Jesus is!**

"The Earth is The Lord's and the fullness thereof, the world and they that dwell therein." Jesus is seated on the right hand of God The Father and the world is His footstool. A wise individual will accept this truth and do whatever it takes to come to Jesus and receive His blessings and protection. He is the only answer to the ailments of humanity. Satan is doing his best to gain as much company in Hell as possible. Remember the old saying, "Misery loves company?" Satan is a defeated foe who lost the battle when Jesus died on the cross and rose from the dead. With the plan of salvation fully activated, Satan knows that his days are limited and he's actively trying to divert people from Jesus with deceit, lies and treachery. If you wake up in Hell it'll be too late and once there you're stuck. Satan will laugh at you throughout all eternity regarding how you fell for his parlor tricks and gimmicks!

No matter what others will try to tell you, Jesus Christ is the only way out of this life into an eternity of safety and security. No matter who is the occupant of The White House, only faith in Jesus Christ will deliver you from the evil of this world. The person in The White House cannot save you from sin nor save your eternal soul. They can only deal with our temporal state and our temporal issues. Issues which pale in comparison to eternal issues. Issues which bear no importance in comparison to the creation and sustaining of a relationship with our Lord and Savior Jesus Christ. A relationship with Him guarantees eternal success, anything else guarantees eternal failure. Many will be deceived and many will just plainly reject the idea that there is a God, He has a Son named Jesus Christ and that there is a life after this one. Heaven is the place that I want to make my home. I want happiness for all eternity and I have changed my behavior so that my desire will become a reality. I want this for my wife, I want this for my daughter and I especially want this for you!

I fully understand that life behind bars is not the life you want for yourself. Jesus Christ can change your life for the better. You have to educate yourself as to who He is and what He can do for you, by reading His Holy Word. Familiarize yourself with the scriptures. Pray multiple times throughout the day so that you can enhance your relationship with Him. Divorce yourself from bad activities and bad influences and ask Him for His help. He will strengthen your resolve if you ask Him to. He will lighten your load if you convert your current lifestyle to His lifestyle. He will make changes in your life that you thought were impossible, but, there is nothing impossible for Him!

My friend, I humbly ask of you to ask God Almighty to come into your heart and reconstruct your life. Let Him know that you are sorry for your sins and you wish to repent. Ask Him to change your status quo. Ask Him to protect you from satanic influences and ask Him to deliver you from the evil of this world. Belief in Him is not the end, it is the beginning. Live for Jesus and His light will undoubtedly shine in you and through you. Once Papa Jesus has become an active part of your life, people will recognize the change. This change will intimidate some and infuriate others. This is to be expected because everyone that you know does not truly wish you well. Many smile in your face and jump for joy behind your back when disaster strikes in your general direction. Also, many are either too prideful, too egotistic or too cowardly to declare Jesus Christ as Lord Of All!

Your relationship with Papa Jesus will cause some to hate and despise you and others will just completely leave you alone. That's okay because those who hate and despise will reap the benefits of hate. As you continue on your Christian journey, you will eventually see that a large number of people just flat out hate God and despise anyone associated with Him. They would rather believe in the fallible science of man instead of the infallibility of our Heavenly Father. You will definitely run into those who choose to oppose Christ. Stand your ground and let them know that your faith is stable, unshakable and unbreakable. What happened yesterday was just the tip of the iceberg in regards to what is to come. Living a Christian lifestyle will always reap **Eternal** benefits. Everything else, is for the Hell-bound and foolish. That's not you, right? Remember this as you walk with God, and once again, Happy New Year!

Sincerely,

Brother Griff

CHAPTER SIX

~

Stamina & Endurance

January 27th, 2021

Dear Friend,

Greetings! In the name of our Lord and Savior Jesus Christ I write to you today to wish you God's eternal blessings. I hope that you are faring well in your current environment. I would like to ask you to do me a favor. I would like for you to write to me and tell me about your daily schedule. I would like to know what takes place during the course of an average day with you from lights on to lights out. It is my desire to get a better understanding of your routine which would thereby give me a better understanding of exactly what you go through and what you endure!

Endurance is something that we all need more of. The ability to endure is one of the essential building blocks of human existence. Anyone involved in any type of activity has to be able to rely upon their stamina in order to help them to achieve their goals and objectives. As a youngster, I was involved in many sports. One of my favorites was Track & Field. I ran Track for a local recreation center and participated in the city championships many times and in multiple events. One year I was the city champion, for my age group, in the 50 yard dash. While at those events, I would watch the bigger kids compete in the long distance races like the one mile and two mile races and relays. Being a sprinter, I was amazed at how those kids could run for so long. When I asked how these people could run like that, I then learned about stamina and endurance!

Stamina is what you develop in order to do something for a prolonged period of time.

When children first learn how to walk, they use anything available to help them stand up. Once upright, they try to walk as long and as far as their little legs can endure. Their stamina hasn't been built up to the point where they can walk far, but, those first few steps that they took inspired them to do it again. Before long, due to persistence, they become toddlers. Then the miracle begins because after they learn how to walk, they learn how to run. Starting off crawling, advancing to walking, ending up running. In each phase, the amount of stamina that the child has is minimal because they are just starting out. The more they practice and the more they persist, their stamina develops, grows and modifies. This growth, development and modification is where endurance is born!

Let's take this example and apply it to Christianity. When you accept Jesus Christ as your Lord and Savior, you have now joined His Track Team. At this primary stage, your stamina and endurance is very low. You are now endeavoring to run a good race for The Lord. Death is our finish line and Heaven is our reward. The race is not easy and at times it will seem like you are running uphill and against the wind. There will be times when you will feel like stopping and just plain giving up. Don't think that you are the only one that feels this way. It happens to all of us. This is the key point where stamina and endurance kick in!

My Freshman year in high school, I joined the Track Team. I sprinted in three events and did the long jump. At the first track meet of the season I damaged my Achilles Tendon long jumping. The pain was so intense that I was forced to quit the team. At the last track meet of the season, I returned to try my hand at the 330 yard low hurdles. The track meet was at La Jolla High School. Long story short, I finished dead last. I'd never finished dead last in a race in my life. I was mortified and vowed to return to Track & Field when I had fully recovered!

I stayed away from organized sports my Sophomore year and returned to the Track Team my Junior year. I decided to leave field events alone and placed all of my emphasis on sprinting. I ran the 100 yard & 220 yard dashes, I was the anchor man of the 440 yard relay and I was determined to conquer the 330 yard low hurdles. At La Jolla High School, I ran the low hurdles against 3 guys who were almost 1 foot taller than me. Nevertheless, I was completely redeemed in that race and not only did I win the race in a grand fashion, I broke the school record in the low hurdles doing it!

God knew how badly I wanted to be able to compete again. Becoming injured really put a strain on my psyche, stamina and endurance. Dealing with an injured Achilles Tendon, I could barely walk, more or less run. It seemed as though my days of Track & Field were over, yet God had other plans for me. What I thought versus what God knew, were two completely different things. I prayed for things to get better for me and The Lord heard my prayer. He gave me the stamina to get through my recovery phase and the endurance to rejoin the team after a one year hiatus. And the rest was history. I outscored everyone else on our Track Team and finished the season having scored 69.75 points overall. I received my very first trophy in life, Most Valuable Athlete/MVP, and I was ecstatic!

It would have been very easy for me to have simply given up after my injury, yet God had other plans for me. One of my older brothers was the MVP of our Track Team in 1969 and I was the MVP in 1979. He reached that status as a High School Senior and Papa Jesus allowed me to achieve that status as a High School Junior. Papa Jesus alone made this possible for me! Not me, not myself and not I. Papa Jesus planted the seeds in my heart not only to heal, but to be able to return to one of my favorite sports and excel in that sport the way that He wanted me to. My father had died in April of my Sophomore year. It was the most devastating tragedy that I have endured in my lifetime. My father was the best friend that I've ever had. As a child, my daddy would take me to my Saturday track meets and sometimes he would be able to attend the City Championships hosted at Balboa Stadium. Although Papa Jesus had called him home to be with Him, I knew that my daddy was watching over me when I had the most prolific and successful Track & Field season of my life. I have dedicated all praise, glory and honor to Papa Jesus for that miraculous Track & Field season.

It was a season of hard work, physical and mental redemption, wonderful memories and completely unexpected successes/achievements. God gave me the determination, the stamina and the endurance, not only to recover from my injuries, but, to accomplish feats on the Track Team that I never imagined would be possible for me!

Hebrews chapter 12 verse 1 says this;

"Wherefore seeing that we also are compassed about with so great a cloud of witnesses, let us weigh aside every weight, and the sin which doth so easily beset us, and let us run with patience the race that is set before us."

We are all, therefore, running the race of life. Birth is our starting line and death is the finish line. However, if you remember what the goal is, eternal life in the Kingdom Of Heaven, you will work to develop your stamina in order to increase your endurance. The Lord wants all of us to be able to endure what Satan relentlessly throws at us. He constantly is attempting to trip us up along the way, so that we give up and just say forget it and quit. God wants all of us to cross that finish line and claim the victory that awaits all Christians. Keeping your eyes on the prize will aid you in developing more stamina and endurance!

Praying to The Lord and asking Him to strengthen your resolve and draw you closer to Him, will ultimately enhance your overall being. Bible study will grant you much more knowledge of who Our Savior is and what He is capable of. This knowledge will propel you towards a stronger ability to run a good race. Just starting out as a Christian also means that your stamina is low. Working to increase your knowledge of Jesus and deepening your relationship with Him changes that. This is why putting on the whole armor of Christ is so very important. You must remember that you have made the decision to join His team, therefore, you must work towards your goals and play the game by His rules!

His rules dictate that you love thy neighbor and divorce yourself from those who choose evil over good. Those who choose darkness over light. His rules dictate that you will leave alcohol and drugs alone and conduct your life with a clear head and a clear mind. His rules dictate that you will not lie, kill or steal. His rules dictate that you will not curse when you speak and that you refrain from impure thoughts. His rules dictate that you will place Him first in your life and nothing else. Not money, not power, not drugs, not anything!

Jesus will give you stamina and endurance if you do the work and ask, through the power of prayer, for strength, guidance and protection. Placing Him as the centerpiece of your life will change your life for the better if you are willing to change your life from the worst. With the environment that you are currently in, this will not make you popular, but it will make you SAVED! Conviction to Him is the best form of conviction ever, because the benefits are eternal!

Papa Jesus wants a better relationship with you. He wants you to thrive and be able to run a good race. Enhance your stamina and endurance by living the way He wants you to live. Prayer is the key building block of developing a better, deeper and more personal relationship with Our Lord and Savior Jesus Christ. God knows what is in your heart, however, He wants to hear you verbalize your hopes, needs and desires. Prayer is one of the communicative mediums through which Papa Jesus operates. He wants to hear from you and loves it when you open up your heart to Him. Build up your knowledge, stamina and endurance by reading His word, living His lifestyle and obeying His laws. Tell others what Jesus has done for you and spread the word of His love, generosity and mercy. Don't keep it to yourself, talk to those who want to learn about Him and read The Bible together. Let the love of Jesus Christ be seen in you by your thoughts, words and actions. What you do for Jesus will stand the test of time, everything else will fall. Knowing that, what are you prepared to do? God Bless you my friend!

Sincerely,

Brother Griff

CHAPTER SEVEN

Our Greatest Foe

February 25th, 2021

Dear Friend,

In the name of our Lord & Savior Jesus Christ I bear you the warmest of greetings. I would like to spend time today speaking about our greatest foe. That foe is none other than Satan. Created as Lucifer, he was the angel of light. It was said that his utter beauty was only second to the beauty of Almighty God Himself. A fact that was repeated in Heaven many times. I personally believe that vanity was ultimately the sin that lead to his eventual downfall.

When man was created, Lucifer was informed that man, unlike angels, had been given an eternal soul. You see, angels had been created as immortals, yet man, being encased in flesh, was given an eternal soul. This soul now placed man on an equal if not higher status with angels by Almighty God The Father because God created man in His image. What ultimately infuriated Lucifer was the fact that God wanted the angels to be His messengers to man. Lucifer felt that since the angels were tasked with watching over mankind, therefore, man should worship angels and not God. Basically, Lucifer wanted to be worshiped as a god himself. He personally lead a revolt against God and one third of all the angels sided with Lucifer and rebelled against Almighty God!

Lucifer decided that in order to get back at God, he would lead the attack against those that God especially loved, namely mankind. His second act of rebellion was to deceive Eve into breaking God's one and only law for mankind. Eating that forbidden fruit. He deceived Eve into believing that if she ate the forbidden fruit, she wouldn't die, she would be just as smart as God is. She took the bait and fell into the trap. Soon thereafter, she told Adam, and he fell into the same trap!

God soon discovered their sin and cursed mankind, the Earth and the animal kingdom for this display of disobedience. For this reason, we now get sick and fall victim to illness & disease. Our days are numbered, greatly reduced and we eventually die. For most animals, in order for one animal to live, another animal must die. Animals have fear or antipathy towards man and in order for man to eat, he must labor in order to feed himself. Women have great pain when giving birth and snakes were cursed to slither on their belly and eat only of the dust of their mouths. God placed enmity, which means animosity, between man & the animal kingdom, especially snakes. Additionally, animals may no longer speak to man like they did in the days of the garden. We now have weeds and the Earth is difficult to cultivate. Dust invades our homes & workplaces and our relationship with our Creator was forever severed!

Satan couldn't be happier. He has brought discord between God and man and now he seeks to keep the disharmony flowing. Satan loves to deceive, misdirect and confuse. Fear is one of his favorite tools as well as ignorance. He wants to keep the discord between God and man going forever. Unfortunately for Satan, God had a plan. God would send His only begotten son to pay the debt for a sinful mankind. Satan tried to stop this but he failed. Jesus was born of The Virgin Mary, lived among man for 33 years and died on the cross, thereby, establishing the plan of salvation. He rose on the third day with all power in his hands and ascended into Heaven where He is seated on the right hand of God The Father, making divine intercession for those who believe in Him!

Satan now knows that he is running out of time. The Church is the bride of Christ and we are quickly approaching the end of the Church age. After that will be The Rapture, The Tribulation and then The Second Coming of Our Lord and Savior. When Papa Jesus comes again, Satan knows that he will be chained up and locked away in a bottomless pit for no less than 1000 years. This is why Satan does not want you to read the Book Of Revelation. His fate is manifested in this book and he doesn't want you to know about it. He wants to keep you ignorant of how he eventually gets dealt with!

He uses the same old trickery, deceit, lies, confusion and false promises, to lure God's children away from him. Satan represents darkness, Papa Jesus is the way, the truth and the life. Jesus Christ is the light of the world. Satan is a defeated foe who is only interested in deceiving as many souls as possible into joining him in eternal damnation. Remember back in the garden of Eden when he appeared to Eve as a snake? If you know anything about snakes, when you cut off their head, their body still thrashes around until it finally dies. Satan's head was cut off when Jesus died on the cross. However, his body is still thrashing about in an attempt to wreak as much havoc as possible before The Second Coming. He is a defeated foe, whose only concern is to trick you into sharing his fate. Why, because misery loves company!

Do not be deceived! Jesus is the light of the world and Satan is the prince of darkness. Look at those around you and ask yourself this question, are they aligned with the light or with darkness? As I have told my daughter since she was in Kindergarten; **"You are who you hang around."** And, **"Birds of a feather, flock together."** Look at who you keep company with and you tell me, is this a Heaven-bound crowd or a Hell-bound crowd? Satan does not want you to escape his grasp. He is the prince of this world and wishes to thwart any attempt you make towards eternal salvation. He knows that he is destined for damnation, and, misery loves company. Never forget that. **Misery Loves Company!**

Reassess your family, reassess your friends and reassess your foes. If they are aligned with this world and not God's Heavenly Kingdom, divorce yourself from them. **Immediately!** Romans chapter 16 verses 17 through 20 states:

17. Now I beseech you brethren, mark them which cause divisions and offenses contrary to the doctrine which ye have learned; and avoid them.

18. For they that are such serve not our Lord Jesus Christ, but their own belly; and by good words and speeches deceive the hearts of the simple.

19. For your obedience is come abroad unto all men. I am glad therefore on your behalf: but yet I would have you wise unto that which is good, and simple concerning evil.

20. And the God of peace shall bruise Satan under your feet shortly. The grace of our Lord Jesus Christ be with you. Amen.

Paul was speaking in a letter to the Romans in those verses. He was basically telling the members of the early Christian Church to watch who they hang around and avoid those who preach a false doctrine. Those who attempt to lead you down the wrong path will be divinely dealt with soon enough. People will talk a good game but, upon closer scrutiny, you will see that their actions are out of sync with their words. **In other words, they do not practice what they preach.** As you go through this life, look around and see for yourself how often this is the case with people who claim to be your friends, and furthermore, claim to be Christians. Therefore, you must be very mindful of exactly who you associate yourself with and who you choose to hang around!

Your eternal soul is much more important than friendships, kin-ships, loose lips and sinking ships! Divorcing yourself from bad influences will definitely make you unpopular to those that you thought had nothing but love for you. They will claim that you have changed. **And you have changed!** When you consciously change directions in life from walking in darkness to walking in light, it can't help but become evident to everyone around you. You have wisely and intelligently let Papa Jesus into your heart and now it shows! The New Testament confirms this in 1 Peter chapter 4 verses 14 through 16 which states:

14. If ye be reproached for the name of Christ, happy are ye, for the spirit of glory and of God resteth upon you: on their part he is evil spoken of, but on your part he is glorified.

15. But let none of you suffer as a murderer, or as a thief, or as an evildoer, or as a busybody in other men's matters.

16. Yet if any man suffer as a Christian, let him not be ashamed; but let him glorify God on this behalf.

Some folks will claim that you act like you are too good to be around them anymore, and furthermore, they'll claim that you act like you are holier than thou. Your response to that should be: **"That you are not holier than thou, you are just blessed right now!"** I distinctly remember being accused of this when I stopped drinking alcohol in 1987. People will despise you for attempting to change for the better and will rejoice when you fail in your attempts to do so. The book of Job chapter 8 verse 22 says this:

"They that hate thee shall be clothed with shame; and the dwelling place of the wicked shall come to nought."

This basically means that those who despise you for trying to better yourself will reap what they sow. Always remember that God said: **"Vengeance is mine, I shall repay."** Those are some very strong words coming from a very powerful God. Many will try to persuade you that there is no such thing as God. There is more evidence that proves that there is a God, than there is that disproves it. Just look up at the sky at nighttime. Do you really believe that all of what you see in the nighttime sky was created because a piece of matter the size of a pin head exploded? If that is indeed the case, then who created that tiny piece of matter? Furthermore, who caused that tiny piece of matter to explode? Satan created this ridiculous ideology to stand in opposition to God's factual account of creation. Satan is the catalyst for this despicable conduct. Satan loves to deceive and do everything possible to oppose and discredit God's word. Our greatest foe is Satan and those who align themselves with darkness who gladly choose to do his bidding. Embrace the blessings and the changes that come with commitment to Jesus Christ. Now is the time to make Papa Jesus the centerpiece of your life. Your soul will thank you, eternally!

Sincerely,

Brother Griff

CHAPTER EIGHT

Divide & Conquer

March 31st, 2021

Dear Friend,

I n the name of our Lord & Savior Jesus Christ I would like to greet you and let you know that God is watching over you. Although you are incarcerated, you are surviving in the most difficult and stressful of environments. You could very easily have become a victim of your surroundings and become another statistic of the penal system. Have you ever thought why you have survived when you have witnessed so much death, villainy and pure evil? The answer is; **The Will Of God!**

God is sitting on His throne and He has the whole world in His hands. Nothing happens in this world without His permission. God is watching over you and He and He alone is solely responsible for your absolute safety in such a harsh and hazardous environment. Satan understands this completely. He loves to use the classic **Divide And Conquer** technique to enhance his ranks and deceive the gullible and recruit the soft and the hardcore unbelievers. Don't believe me, then let's go back to where it all began. Let's go all the way back to the beginning when he decided to rebel against Almighty God The Father!

His first act of **Divide And Conquer** was when he decided to rebel against his creator, Almighty God The Father. He felt that mankind should pray to and worship him since God The Father had tasked the angels with watching over man. Satan, being the angel of light, fell victim to his own vanity. Vanity being the sin that ultimately led to his rebellion and downfall. Satan voiced his displeasure with God and one third of the angels in Heaven sided with him. They were therefore subsequently cast out of Heaven and forced to reside outside of God

The Father's Kingdom. His rebellion divided a unified Heavenly population and a unified host of angels and turned them into two competing factions, angels versus demons, phase one!

His second act of **Divide And Conquer** was when he decided to come between God and man. He deceived Eve by tricking her into believing that she wouldn't die if she ate the forbidden fruit. He told her that if she ate of the tree of knowledge of good and evil, she would become just as smart as God The Father. That was the first act of division between God and Mankind. Satan deceived Eve into sin which completed phase two. Eve therefore told Adam and convinced him that he wouldn't die either. Adam ate the fruit as well and that completed phase three. Satan had officially come between God The Father and the only creation that He had made in His own image. This act of insubordination and disobedience got man kicked out of the Garden Of Eden and forever changed the course of history for mankind!

Satan was overjoyed! He had successfully deceived innocent and gullible man into disobeying his creator, God The Father. Man was now separated from God and with God now angry with mankind, Satan could now enjoy phase four of his **Divide And Conquer** strategy. Man was forced to leave paradise and fend for himself. Yet our God is a merciful God so He sent angels to watch over mankind and instruct man in basic survival skills such as; planting crops, cultivation, carpentry, irrigation, mathematics, hunting, masonry, harvesting crops, food preparation and construction. These angels, in the book of Genesis chapter 6, were referred to as; "Sons of God," and they too eventually sinned against God The Father by taking wives of the daughters of man which they themselves chose without God's permission. The children of this sinful and unsanctioned union were referred to as; **"Mighty men, which were of old, men of renown."** God was grieved that he had made man and in the 6th chapter of the book of Genesis, God decided to destroy the world!

Let's take a look at this. Genesis chapter 1 depicts creation, with man being created on the sixth day. Genesis chapter 2 depicts the creation of Eve, life in the Garden Of Eden and its geographic location. Unfortunately, by the time you get through the 3rd chapter of Genesis, man has disobeyed and broken the only rule that God had given Him and subsequently managed to get himself kicked out of paradise. How dreadfully tragic and ironic. But wait, Genesis chapter 4 depicts the the birth of the first siblings in history, and also, the very first murder. A murder committed by the older brother, Cain, against the younger brother, Abel. The seeds of dysfunction within the very first family unit had not only been planted, but now bore its first fruits. Man had murdered man and brother had murdered brother. Phase five was now complete!

Satan had successfully rebelled against God, reduced the population of angels by one third, caused the division of man from God, was the architect of the very first eviction in history, upset the harmony of the very first marriage and created dysfunction between the world's first pair of siblings, resulting in the first murder in history. And this is what Satan accomplished within the first four chapters of the book of Genesis. This is just the first book of The Holy Bible. Satan had been so busy with his **Divide And Conquer** strategy, that by the time you get to Genesis chapter 7, God destroys the Earth with The Great Flood! Can you blame Him?

Satan loves to **Divide And Conquer.** It has been adopted as a classic military strategy throughout the history of mankind. Deception leads to separation between man and God, between husband and wife, between siblings and between friends. Once a unified group has been deceived, it is much easier for Satan to manipulate and attack half of them instead of all of them. This is a perfect example of cutting your enemy down to size. Isn't it easier to fight five battles instead of ten? Repeat the process enough times and your victims will start to add up. Satan loves to deceive because it is the oldest weapon in his arsenal and deceit always leads to division!

So now lets bring this all back to you. At some point in time, you learned about right and wrong. Somewhere along the line, someone convinced you that criminality would get you closer to your goals in life, faster than punching a clock. Do you now see, that a demon was whispering those sentiments into your ears and not an angel? Do you now see, that you yourself have become a statistic in Satan's **Divide And Conquer** strategy? Are you currently with your family, your friends and your loved ones? Sadly, the answer is no! Are you currently able to come and go as you please, or are you currently under the scrutiny and regimentation of the penal system? Looking back at your life, someone or something, deceived you, so that you began to make bad life choices. **Divide And Conquer!** We all make mistakes, however, your mistakes have cost you your freedom. I don't wish that on anyone!

The redeeming quality of this is that you can still choose to follow God. Doing this will cause you to act, talk, walk and interact differently.

Seeking the Christian lifestyle will always cause a change for the better in your life. Papa Jesus always watches over His own. His will shall never be thwarted. Satan is operating on borrowed time and he knows that his time is quickly running out. He knows that he is a defeated foe and that the only individuals that he can truly conquer are the foolish. This is why you see so much chaos and confusion running rampant in the world today!

Satan's **Divide And Conquer** strategy can be seen every time you pick up a newspaper or watch the evening news. Look at how much chaos you see erupting all over the globe, **Divide And Conquer!** Look at how Black men are being murdered by the police on an unprecedented level, **Divide And Conquer!** So are we to assume that being non-white is now the probable cause for criminal behavior? Take a good look at the racial makeup of our penal system and you answer that question for me. Do you see more **justice or Just-Us? Divide And Conquer!** The process of the Criminalization of;

skin color, socioeconomic status, race, ethnicity, educational levels, homelessness, unemployment, religious beliefs and cultural differences, are just a few more examples of Satan's **Divide And Conquer** strategy!

When you criminalize people for being homeless, for being poor, for being non-white, for being uneducated, for being unemployed, for having a different religion or for being a member of a different culture, you have subsequently divided a unified body of humanity and conquered them through criminal prosecution. Second class citizenship should never be tolerated and yet we see it being manifested worldwide on a daily basis. It leads to mayhem, violence, murder and genocide. Look at how the rich manage to get richer and the poor are definitely getting poorer, **Divide And Conquer!** Look at how large corporations and billionaires hardly pay any taxes at all whereas the middle-class is rapidly shrinking and becoming a thing of the past. **Divide And Conquer!** Do you see more hypocrisy taking place in the world today or less? **Divide And Conquer!**

Satan is attempting **The Jedi Mind-Trick** on a planetary level. If you have not **Put On The Whole Armor Of Jesus Christ,** you too can fall victim to his devious attempts to deceive. Satan is a master of deception and he loves to continue to do so because it is his preferred weapon of choice. **Deceive, Manipulate, Divide, Conquer and Repeat!** Satan has done this day after day, year after year, decade after decade, century after century, millennium after millennium. No wonder he's good at it, just look at how long he's had to perfect his craft! Also, look how busy he has been since he was kicked out of Heaven. You saw how busy he was in the first six chapters of the Book Of Genesis. He is even busier now because Satan knows that he is quickly running out of time!

Love will always conquer hate and God is love. God has and will allow Satan to run amuck for the present, but it won't last. God has you right where you need to be right now. At this point in your life, He has your full and complete attention. Read your Bible and increase your knowledge of exactly who God is and what He is capable of. Pray to our Heavenly Father so that He will make you aware of Satan's deceptive and divisive tactics. Ask The Lord to give you heightened awareness of Satan's gimmicks and tricks. Ask Papa Jesus for His continued protection everyday and thank Him for all blessings received. Ask Him to fortify your soul and make you more resistant to satanic bombardment. Thank Him for protecting you in the worst of environments. Thank Him for sparing you, when others around you drop like flies. Thank Him for the mercy that He provides to those who simply turn toward Him and away from Satan!

Jesus loves you my friend and that is why he has made you a survivor and not a statistic. Rejoice in The Lord and know that He will always have your back! There is no situation that He cannot fix and there is no jam that He can't get you out of. Please read your Bible on a daily basis and pray to Papa Jesus as your schedule permits. He will bring you through these difficult days and He has reserved a home for you in His Eternal Kingdom. Please praise His holy name and thank Him for watching over you and keeping you safe in an unsafe world. God bless you my friend!

Sincerely,

Brother Griff

CHAPTER NINE

———— ∾ ————

Trouble & Adversity

May 24th, 2021

Dear Friend,

I wish you God's greatest blessings on this new day! I hope that you have been faring well. Today I would like to draw your attention to a passage from the book of Job in the Old Testament. Job chapter 14 verses one and two says this:

1. Man that is born of a woman is of few days, and full of trouble.

2. He cometh forth like a flower, and is cut down: He fleeth also as a shadow, and continueth not.

This pair of verses completely epitomizes the state of man on this Earth since he was evicted from The Garden Of Eden. No man has ever walked this Earth without being troubled by something or someone. Even our Lord And Savior Jesus Christ saw plenty of trouble during His thirty three years on Earth. You yourself can plainly see that, as you look back at your life, there have been times of trouble. Do you know of anyone that has claimed that they have not had one day of trouble in their lives? I don't think so. Trouble is a very common thing and no one is immune to it!

People often think that if they were rich, all of their troubles would just melt away. Trust me, they might be able to pay off all of their bills, but, their troubles have just begun. When you're poor, nobody cares about your money because they know that you don't have any. When you're rich, everybody is trying to count your money in the attempts to try to get a piece of it. Poor folks can go wherever they want to in peace and nobody cares. As soon as a rich or famous person walks out of their front door, the paparazzi haunt them from start to finish. Don't believe me, just look at what happened to Princess Diana. Such a terrible tragedy! The point is, that trouble will find you no matter who you are and whatever your station in life is. Man had no idea of what trouble was when he lived in The Garden Of Eden. He walked and talked with Almighty God on a daily basis. He had no knowledge of what struggle and strife was. Doubt, fear and trouble, was completely nonexistent, because, Almighty God was there with him at all times. Unfortunately, when man decided to break the one and only rule that God had given him, man learned very quickly about trouble!

Since man managed to get himself kicked out of paradise, you can easily say that the name of our own shadow is trouble. Trouble follows us with each and every step we take. Trouble knows your name, your address and your phone number. How many times has this been your testimony? You were having a great day until your phone rang or until you answered your doorbell. How many times have you checked your email only to find drama awaiting you online? Trouble knows when you clocked in on your job and exactly when you clocked out. Trouble knows exactly when to pay you a visit and when it is least welcome in your life. Trouble surrounds you when you're on the freeway and goes with you on vacation. Trouble knows how to turn a sweet dream into a nightmare and how to transform joy into despair. Trouble knows how to ruin a nice day and how to make a bad day worse. Along with his sidekicks, fear and doubt, trouble knows how to make good times bad and bad times miserable. It is safe to say that trouble is what we inherited ever since man disobeyed God!

I love to have a good time, just like everyone else, but it seems that trouble is attracted to laughter and smiles. Trouble can't stand them and trouble loves to turn them into tears and frowns. If I had a dollar for every time I went to a gathering and uninvited guests who decided to crash the party ruined the whole thing, I'd be a very rich man. Trouble is Satan's playground and he loves to drag us all into it and make us stay for a while. Satan hates love, joy and happiness. He prefers hate, suffering and pain. Satan knows that trouble is the platform that he can operate on in order to deceive, manipulate and coerce man into following his path towards destruction. All the while, Satan will fool you into believing that you are doing what makes you feel good when, in reality, he is manipulating you into doing that which is contrary to God's law. That, my friend, is exactly how you get tricked, duped and fooled into following Satan's path and not God's path. A path which is the essence of truly getting into trouble. Many are roasting in Hell today because they were tricked into false beliefs and false doctrines that led them directly to the gates of Hell. Now, unfortunately, they realize exactly how wrong they were and now they will pay the price for their foolishness eternally. Trouble, is one of Satan's favorite weapons in his arsenal, and, as long as we are alive, Satan will target us with trouble at every opportunity. However, another name for trouble is adversity and adversity is God's proving ground for Christians. Let me explain!

God knows that man is a weak creature. Jesus himself told us that; **"The spirit is willing, but the flesh is weak."** Being encased in flesh, how do you strengthen the spirit? Through adversity. It is said that God will never give you more than you can bear. Adversity, therefore, is the gymnasium where Christians get their spiritual workout. Trouble comes and trouble goes. Adversity is God's way of testing and measuring exactly where we are mentally, spiritually and physically. Imagine adversity as being an obstacle course and Satan is in charge of placing the potholes, landmines, man-traps and other various obstacles in our path. Successfully completing this obstacle course has an eternal reward of salvation and everlasting life in the Kingdom Of Heaven. In addition to spiritual growth! Failing this obstacle course has an eternal punishment of never-ending torment in Hell!

Once you decide to give your life to The Lord, the hunt is on. You will be targeted by Satan, just like Job, to be the object of his persecution. Satan will throw everything at you, including the kitchen sink. Calling on The Lord, during these times of stress and anxiety, will demonstrate spiritual growth and Christian dedication. Praying to The Lord and asking for guidance, strength and protection, thereby enhances your spirit which subsequently draws you closer to The Lord. When The Lord helps you to overcome a trial or tribulation, you will grow spiritually through your faith in The Lord. This makes adversity God's magnet for drawing His followers closer to Him by strengthening them through trials and tribulations. Otherwise known as adversity. During times of trouble, we are being tested, examined and graded on just how we choose to respond to adversity. If you lean toward The Lord, your spirit strengthens, your dedication is enhanced and your relationship with Papa Jesus grows closer. If you fall back on your old ways, your pre-Christian ways, the way you acted prior to accepting Jesus as your Lord and Savior, you aren't displaying any spiritual growth at all. Lack of spiritual growth equals stagnation at best and regression at worst!

Satan will hate you for accepting Papa Jesus as your Lord and Savior. People who you thought were your friends will show you their true colors. Many will ridicule you and kick you to the curb. Be forewarned and be advised, your existing group of friends will make their true identities known to you when you accept The Lord. Therefore, depart from your sinful ways and choose to live your life for the better. Job chapter 8 verse 22 explains it this way:

"They that hate thee shall be clothed with shame; and the dwelling place of the wicked shall come to nought!"

Man's existence, since being ousted from The Garden Of Eden, has been a troubled one. This life that we all live, is not the life that God The Father planned for us. It is, however, the life that we inherited due to the disobedience of Adam and Eve. Faith in Jesus Christ is the golden ticket to The Kingdom Of Heaven. A place of peace, harmony and eternal joy. It is the place that mankind has been striving to return to, ever since Noah's Ark finally landed. Until we get there, trouble will follow us every step of the way!

Trouble is what Satan will throw at you. Adversity is God's magnet to a closer relationship with Him. No matter how you look at it, no matter what you call it, we are all being measured, tested and examined on a daily basis. Until we breathe our last breath, we are all on the great obstacle course of life. We all will know trouble and adversity until the day we die. There is no avoiding it and there definitely is no escaping it. Who you rely on when the going gets tough, will blatantly reveal your spiritual standing with The Lord. What do you do when the going gets tough? Do you call on The Lord or do you act a fool? As soon as you hit a pothole on the road of life, do you act like a Christian or act like a heathen? Ask yourself this, am I closer to God after trouble pays me a visit or farther away? Pray to The Lord for guidance, strength and wisdom as you continue your Christian journey. Call on The Lord and ask Him to protect you from the evil of this world. He will never forsake you!

Sincerely,

Brother Griff

CHAPTER TEN

Blessings To The Reader

June 1st, 2021

Dear Friend,

May the grace of our Lord and Savior Jesus Christ surround you on this new day. I sincerely hope and pray that this letter finds you doing well. Today is the first day of June and I am ever so amazed at exactly how fast time is moving on. It seems as if we were celebrating the new year just a few days ago and now here we are in June, the midpoint of the year 2021. God has been very good to me and His grace, mercy and blessings have manifested themselves to my family and I on a daily basis!

When this year started off, our world was still in a state of crisis due to the Covid-19 pandemic. Now, as I write this letter, over half of the adult population of The United States Of America have been fully vaccinated. In comparison to last year at this point in time, that is truly a miracle. There are more people out on the streets now and the freeways are starting to look more and more like they did 2 years ago. Small businesses are starting to bounce back and things are beginning to look more usual. Yes, there are still facial coverings on everyone's face and some businesses have completely shut down permanently. However, I have witnessed more hope and optimism in the faces of people now than I have seen for quite awhile. Overall, with the advent of multiple vaccines available to the general public, businesses reopening and schools on the brink of returning to normal in the fall, it feels as if people can see the proverbial light at the end of the tunnel. One can easily look around and think of the song, "Happy Days Are Here Again!"

Jesus Christ has this whole wide world in His hands. Nothing ever happens without His approval and He has dominion over all of His creation. Covid-19 is just another example of prophecy being fulfilled. We have lost millions of people to this pandemic and I do not mean to diminish the significance of each and every life lost. I am sorry that people have suffered the loss of not only one, but two, three and sometimes four generations of family members due to this wicked disease. News broadcasts of the past year have had very little to smile about, however, you can draw comfort from the words of Papa Jesus when He declared that, **"This too shall pass."** Just as Almighty God has allowed this global pandemic to take place and fulfill prophecy, He and He alone, will remove it from our presence. As a matter of principle, we should collectively join hands and give thanks to Almighty God that we, the survivors, were not affected worse than we were!

God has been so good to us and this global pandemic has been a constant reminder that we haven't seen anything yet. Covid-19 has been a line drawn in the sand to illustrate the difference between the good old days and the face of what is to come. The Holy Bible tells us that there will be many unprecedented events which will definitely take place prior to The Rapture,

The Tribulation and The Second Coming Of Our Lord And Savior Jesus Christ. The Book Of Revelation, therefore, is the most important book of The Holy Bible when speaking in terms of contemporary relevance. It is a complete and total depiction of where things are going and exactly what will transpire in the future. Everything that God has ever said will happen has indeed come to pass. The Book Of Revelation relays God's knowledge of future events to Saint John The Divine and is the only book of The Holy Bible that guarantees a blessing to the reader. This is the case not only once but twice within this book of future prophecy!

Revelation chapter 1 verse 3 states this:

"Blessed is he that readeth, and they that hear the words of this prophecy, and keep those things which are written therein: for the time is at hand."

This lets you know that you have entered into an elite level of knowledge. God wants each of us to be fully aware of what is to come. Reading this book will completely remove the "Oh, I didn't know..." excuse from everyone's mouth and subsequently bless you for desiring to deepen your knowledge of God's future plans. Remember when I stated that this book contains two blessings for the reader? Revelation chapter 22 verses 6 and 7 states this:

6. "And He said unto me, These sayings are faithful and true: and The Lord God of the holy prophets sent His angel to shew unto His servants the things which must shortly be done.

7. Behold, I come quickly: blessed is he that keepeth the sayings of the prophecy of this book."

Many false prophets blatantly avoid teaching and preaching out of The Book Of Revelation because they fear the truth of what is to come. The Holy Bible is the word of God. You cannot selectively pick and choose what you will believe and what you won't. It doesn't work that way. If your preacher isn't teaching repentance, acceptance of Jesus Christ as Lord and Savior, baptism and revelation knowledge, then please go find another preacher!

The Holy Bible is not only the best selling book in the history of literature but it is, without a doubt, the most misinterpreted. Any person with a dubious agenda can take and twist God's Holy Word to fit their own personal desires. Beware of this, for Jesus stated that in the last days many false prophets will arise and many will be deceived. You must therefore read The Bible on your own so that you yourself will be able to differentiate between true scripture and false doctrine. Many false prophets will lead you down a satanic path because they wish to divert the unknowing into the trap of biblical misinformation. **Do not let this be you!** Reading God's Word with an open mind and a pure heart will allow The Holy Spirit to enter your heart and lead you to the truth!

Our God is a wonderful God, however, He will only give you so long to come to your senses and acknowledge Him as Lord and Savior. Covid-19 is just the tip of the iceberg of what is to come. The age of The Church is rapidly coming to a close and the time of The Rapture is at hand. I beg of you to read The Book Of Revelation and discover for yourself exactly where all of this is going and what the world is leading up to. Thank Almighty God for bringing you through this chaotic point in time and for delivering you to this new and better day. Chronicles chapter 16 verses 34 and 35 says this:

34. "Oh give thanks unto The Lord; For He is good; For His mercy endureth forever.

35. And say ye, save us, O God of our salvation and gather us together, and deliver us from the heathen, that we may give thanks to thy Holy Name, and glory in thy praise."

God is love and God is good. If you are reading this, you have been blessed to be able to state that you have survived the Covid-19 global pandemic thus far. This event has been horrible and yet days are coming that will make you wish for the good old days of Covid-19. Please read The Book Of Revelation at least five times and truly soak up and absorb God's book of future prophecy. The first couple of times that you read it, it may seem confusing. Don't worry, because the more that you read it, the more it will start to make sense. People are afraid of anything that isn't flowery and fluffy and The Book Of Revelation is neither one of those things. The Book Of Revelation is God's play by play endgame for mankind. It pulls no punches and delivers nothing but hard core truth. The question is,

Can you handle the truth? Believers will totally benefit and non-believers shall be destroyed. No ifs, no ands, no buts or maybe. **Hard Core Truth!** The Old Testament books of Daniel and Ezekiel point directly at and lead up to what is covered in the Book Of Revelation. Revelation knowledge is second to none and lets you see exactly what will happen to Satan and his followers. Satan doesn't want you to know what will happen to him. The Book Of Revelation explains exactly what Satan's demise will be. Please read and re-read it. Receive your blessings and become further enlightened! God Bless You!

Sincerely,

Brother Griff

CHAPTER ELEVEN

---~---

Perspective

July 21st, 2021

Dear Friend,

In the name of our Lord and Savior Jesus Christ I bring you greetings. I hope that you are faring well despite your current set of circumstances. As we have now crossed the midpoint of the year 2021, I would like to talk to you today about perspective.

We live in a world of diverse peoples and cultures. What started off as a human population of two, has now grown into a population of billions. Such a large number on such a small planet. It seems as if our planet is getting smaller the more our population increases. Space is at a premium, resources are dwindling, pollution is increasing and the temperatures around the globe are significantly getting warmer. When you take into account the fact that we all must share this planet with our neighbors, you can't help but see that we all don't share the same viewpoint on how to do just that. Governments argue on exactly what needs to be done and all the while this big blue planet just keeps on spinning around and around. Where are we going, why is this happening and what is all of this leading up to?

These are the questions that man has pondered for centuries. I personally believe that the world, as we know it, is bracing itself for some major changes. The more and more that I read The Holy Bible, the more I find that these changes were prophesied centuries ago. Science will explain these events one way whereas faith will explain them another way. What do you think? Do you believe the scientific perspective or do you believe the Biblical perspective? Whatever your answer is, you have a right to see things the way that you see them and you have a right to believe what you believe!

My personal belief is that Papa Jesus is the creator of this universe and that He created time. We exist within this dimension of time and are given a limited amount of it. At the end of our existence in time, we are therefore ushered into the realm of eternity. A dimension that has no ending but has two known locations. One location is Paradise/Heaven and the other location is Hell. Each of these destinations are arrived at due to willful choice. If you choose to believe that Jesus Christ is Lord of all creation, Heaven awaits. If you choose not to believe that Jesus Christ is Lord of all creation, Hell awaits. This, in a nutshell, is the Christian perspective!

Having been created in God's image on the sixth day, man is the only creature mentioned in The Holy Bible that was given an eternal soul. That means that we have a symbiotic relationship between our flesh and our spirit. Each entity has needs, however, the needs of the flesh super-cede the needs of the spirit, in most cases, within the realm of time. The flesh needs food, water, air, clothing, sleep and has a need to reproduce. At first glance, it appears as though the spirit, within the realm of time, is just along for the ride and the flesh calls all of the shots. Unfortunately, for many people who are now experiencing eternal torment in Hell, this was true. A hedonistic life-style coupled with a "Me First" mentality has all too often been the gateway to eternal torment. They did what they felt was the right thing to do according to them and paid no attention to gaining spiritual knowledge. They never tried to learn about God, and if so, they blatantly rejected the notion that there is a God and that He is the sovereign ruler of the universe. However, just the opposite is true!

We were given an eternal soul from our Heavenly Father when we were born. Although encased in flesh, it and it alone will survive the transformation from time to eternity, in other words, from life to death. Our flesh was only cre-ated to dwell within the realm of time, whereas our spirit, which resides within us, was created to reside within the realm of time and flour-ish within the realm of eternity. Our flesh was created and designed to take care of and host our spirit until we are summoned by Papa Jesus to our eternal resting place. Our spirit was created by Almighty God and is His property alone. At the predetermined time, our souls will be required to return to their creator. At that point, a Christian soul will appear at The Judgment Seat Of Christ. The place where Papa Jesus will award and reward us for our works. After this awards ceremony, we will be given A Crown Of Life, access to The Eternal Kingdom Of Heaven, and blessed with eternal joy and happiness!

The soul of the non-believer, however, will appear before Papa Jesus at The Great White Throne Judgment. This is the place where books that recorded every element of your life will be opened and used as evidence against you. Every thought, every word and every action will be held against you. You will be prosecuted to the fullest extent of God's Law and then sentenced to an eternal stay in Hell. The Great White Throne Judgment is not the place that anyone would ever want to be. It is the gateway to eternal torment, in much the same manner as the legal courtroom is to sentencing, being the gateway to prison!

We are creatures of light encased in flesh. Just as the Caterpillar gives way to the Butterfly, so does our Flesh give way to our Spirit. Metamorphosis is our past, present and future state. Perspective, however, is a singular and personal thing. Each person has their own viewpoint, their own set of feelings and their own perspective. I encourage you to take a moment to evaluate your personal outlook and perspective. Knowing what was written in the preceding pages, where does your perspective stand? Do you have a scientific perspective or a Christian perspective? Do you have faith in God or not? Whatever your answer to these questions may be, please know that Jesus loves you. Whether you know Him or not, He does love you tremendously. I hope that this letter will make you think about your personal perspective and motivate you to learn more about our Lord and Savior Jesus Christ!

I am a sinner who has made plenty of mistakes. I have confessed my sins to Papa Jesus and have begged for His forgiveness. My guilt for past sins haunts me because I know the magnitude of what I've done. I hate the things that I've done which have defiled myself and displeased The Lord. When you are truly sorry for your sinful past, you can't help but feel this way. Ezekiel chapter 36 verse 31 sums it up like this:

"Then shall ye remember your own evil ways, and your doings that were not good, and shall loathe yourselves in your own sight for your iniquities and for your abominations."

I do have tremendous guilt, remorse and loathing for my sinful past, however, that guilt becomes nullified when I examine what Papa Jesus did for me at Calvary. All of my sins, past, present & future, were nailed to that cross and left there when I repented, gave my life to Him and was baptized in His Holy Name. I know that Papa Jesus has forgiven me because of how He has blessed me since I've turned my life over to Him. He and He alone has given me the words to write these letters to you in the attempt to enhance your perspective. Acknowledgment of my sins, confession of my sins and repenting of my sins, is what has led me to where I am today. If He could save a wretch like me, He can certainly save you. Ask Him to come into your life and wash away your sinful past so that you can have a victorious future. Belief in Him is the gateway to eternal happiness. You have a right to believe what you want, however, the Christian perspective is the only one that leads to eternal paradise. Knowing that, where do you want to spent eternity? Please read The New Testament of your Bible and see what Papa Jesus did for others and exactly what He can do for you! May God bless you and keep you safe in this unsafe world!

Sincerely,
Brother Griff

Chapter Twelve

A Doubting Thomas

August 5, 2021

Dear Friend,

I am happy to be able to write to you on this blessed new day. I hope and pray that Our Lord and Savior Jesus Christ has been watching over you. I know that being in a state of incarceration is no easy task. Freedom is what all of God's creatures should readily enjoy and for those who have lost their freedom, life can be more difficult than usual. Our Heavenly Father is able to sustain us no matter what our present set of circumstances may be. Faith in Him is the key to a harmonious relationship with Him.

Today I would like to speak about a set of verses from the gospel of Saint John which is the fourth book in The New Testament of The Holy Bible. Saint John chapter 20 verses 24 through 31 says this:

24. But Thomas, one of the twelve, called Didymus, was not with them when Jesus came.

25. The other Disciples therefore said unto him, We have seen the Lord. But he said unto them, Except I shall see in his hands the print of the nails, and put my finger into the print of the nails, and thrust my hand into his side, I will not believe.

26. And after eight days again his disciples were within, and Thomas with them; then came Jesus, the doors being shut, and stood in the midst, and said, Peace be unto you.

27. Then saith he to Thomas, Reach hither thy finger and behold my hands; reach hither

thy hand, and thrust it into my side: and be not faithless, but believing.

28. And Thomas answered and said unto him, My Lord and my God.

29. Jesus saith unto him, Thomas, because thou hast seen me, thou has believed: blessed are they that have not seen, and yet have believed.

30. And many other signs truly did Jesus in the presence of his disciples, which are not written in this book:

31. But these are written, that ye might believe that Jesus is the Christ, the Son of God; and that believing ye might have life through his name.

This set of verses took place after Jesus rose from the dead. In this particular instance, Jesus appeared to His disciples in a room where the doors were locked and the windows were shut. No one but Papa Jesus could just appear within a room that was presumably locked tight. He had appeared to various individuals previously but this was the first time that He appeared to the eleven. Thomas had heard that Jesus had risen from the dead, however, his personal disbelief was made evident in verse 25. Upon seeing Papa Jesus with his own two eyes, in verse 28, he quickly changed his tune. Verse 29 was stated to Thomas but is directed to all of mankind:

"...Blessed are they that have not seen, and yet have believed."

That statement right there is the essence of the Christian faith. At some point in our lives, the name Jesus Christ or God has been mentioned. Maybe you overheard someone having a conversation about religion. Maybe you attended church or Sunday school when you were a child. Whatever the case may be, everyone on this planet has been exposed to God no matter what name was used to describe Him. The Holy Bible states that our God goes by many names and we only know a few of them. Once exposed to that name, a person will naturally ask the question, "Who is that?" After that question has been answered, the individual is left with a personal decision to make. The decision being, "Do I believe this or not?" Belief will spark the desire to learn more about this supernatural entity that created our universe and everything in it including ourselves. Disbelief will kindle rejection. If a person could see God in all of His glory, they couldn't help but believe!

Saul was a man who persecuted Christians in the early days of the church after Jesus ascended back to Heaven. He made sure that Christians were hunted down like dogs and publicly executed. He could easily be described as the Adolf Hitler of his era. One day while traveling down the road to Damascus to continue his persecution of God's people, he was stopped in his tracks and struck with a blinding light. He dropped to his knees because of the sheer brilliance of what he beheld. He then heard a voice which said, **"Saul, Saul, why persecutest thou me?"** This, my friend, was the turning point in his life. He listened to the voice and did exactly what The Lord told him to do. He therefore accepted Jesus Christ as his personal Lord and Savior and subsequently changed his name to Paul. Instead of persecuting Christians, he not only became one, but he went on to write two thirds of the New Testament of The Holy Bible. Upon seeing what God wanted him to see, he saw the error of his ways and devoted the rest of his life to serving Jesus Christ. He went from being the enemy of the faith to being a minister of the faith. He also was an individual who could definitely assert that seeing is believing!

Jesus speaks to all of us. The way He speaks to us will vary from person to person, however, He will give each and every one of us a chance to accept Him as our Lord and Savior. Thomas had a chance to personally see Papa Jesus after He rose from the dead. Saul saw a blinding light which was so brilliant, it literally knocked him off of his feet. For those of us who haven't literally seen him, our charge is to believe in Him sight unseen. Again, I will repeat what is stated in verse 29;

"...Blessed are they that have not seen, and yet have believed"

Thomas doubted that Jesus had risen from the dead. This is where the term **"A Doubting Thomas"** and where the phrase **"Seeing Is Believing"** originated. Some people can be told the truth, however, unless they personally see/witness the truth, they refuse to believe. Thomas had the benefit of being one of the original twelve disciples that Jesus recruited. He therefore was given lenience. We, on the other hand, must walk by faith. Where there is no faith, there is no belief, subsequently, where there is no belief, there is no salvation. Heaven would be much more populated and Hell would be much less populated if everyone was given the lenience that Jesus gave Thomas. Entrance to God's Heavenly Kingdom is based upon faith and belief in Jesus Christ. Eternal damnation is based upon disbelief and rejection of Jesus Christ as Lord and Savior. If you are **"A Doubting Thomas"** you are on the path that leads directly to the gates of Hell. Once you arrive at that destination, **Seeing will be believing!**

The wise individual will take the word of God as is and repent of your sins, get baptized and develop a relationship with Our Lord and Savior. Jesus died on the cross in order that you might have salvation. He gave up His glory so that we may believe in Him and attain His glory. Believers shall be made just like Him and we shall rule with Him. Non-believers shall perish and suffer eternal damnation. Your eternal destination is a matter of choice. Please make the right one! You're not **"A Doubting Thomas"** are you?

Sincerely,

Brother Griff

CHAPTER THIRTEEN

─────── ≈ ───────

Attitude Of Gratitude

October 4, 2021

Dear Friend,

I am happy to greet you today in the name of our Lord and Savior Jesus Christ. Today is the first Monday in the fourth quarter of this new year which is rapidly coming to a close. It seems like just yesterday we were wishing each other "Happy New Year" and now we can see another new year coming up on the horizon. As I look back upon this past year, many thoughts come to mind.

We have seen many events occur that have been news-worthy to say the least. We've seen one president leave The White House and another one get sworn in. We've witnessed a vaccine for the dreaded Covid-19 pandemic make its way from laboratory testing to the general public. Subsequently, we have seen a large portion of the world receive their vaccinations as well as a large population of individuals refuse to get vaccinated for one reason or another. We have witnessed a police officer found guilty for the unjustified murder of Mr. George Floyd which undoubtedly was a first. The world watched as The United States Of America withdrew the last of its troops out of Afghanistan thereby ending America's longest military conflict. We have also seen a dramatic increase in weather phenomena such as hurricanes, floods, firestorms and increasing ocean temperatures, which bear a direct correlation to our worldwide crisis with climate change. Things in some instances seem to be getting better and then things in other instances seem to be getting worse. No matter what I view on the news or hear from other sources, I thank God for constantly and consistently protecting me from the evil in this world.

I am reminded of First Chronicles chapter 16 verses 34 & 35 which reads as follows:

34. O give thanks unto The Lord for He is good; For His mercy endureth forever.

35. And say ye, Save us, O God of our salvation, and gather us together, And deliver us from the heathen, that we may give thanks to thy Holy Name and glory in thy praise.

I am so very thankful that my wife, my daughter and I, have not become another negative statistic in what is becoming an ever-changing world. A world that has become accustomed to wearing masks, social distancing and getting vaccinated, due to the effects of this global pandemic. My wife, my daughter and I, contracted the Original or possibly The U.K. Variant of Covid-19 in December of 2020 prior to the release of the vaccine for our age group. Fortunately, by the grace of God, none of us required hospitalization. My next door neighbor, however, who was only 35 years old, died of the Delta variant in August of this year. I thank God daily for His protection in this tumultuous world of chaos, rebellion, violence, greed, disruption and deceit. We are all victims of our surroundings, however, I can completely declare that The Lord has kept me safe no matter how unsavory my environment was. He has always kept me within a bubble of His protection and I will never doubt His ability to do so. He has always been good to me and he has enabled me to develop and maintain an attitude of gratitude. An attitude that is completely shared by my wife and my daughter. God's grace and mercy has followed me every day of my life. From my conception until I enter His eternal Kingdom, He has shielded me from Satan and his imps of evil.

I am, and forever will be, eternally grateful for everything that The Lord has done for me and for the protection that He has given me, time and time again. I thank God for delivering me from situations and circumstances where I could have been and should have been, a statistic. Throughout my lifetime, my Lord and Savior has delivered me from tragedy, catastrophe and calamity. I've been involved in numerous car accidents and I've walked away from every one of them. I have had a gun pulled out and pointed at me 10 times and was shot at twice. Papa Jesus redirected the trajectory of those bullets so that I was never shot. I have been handcuffed, searched and man-handled by the police but never arrested. Police dogs were sent to sniff out the contents of my Lowrider and they never found a thing. Law enforcement may have pointed guns at me, but, they never planted anything in my car and only due to the grace of God can I state that every traffic stop that I was involved in, always ended peacefully. I have worked on many cars in my lifetime and on 3 occasions the car fell off of the jack/jack stands and The Lord saw to it that, when it happened, I wasn't still underneath the car. When friends of mine got car-jacked, it never happened to me. When encounters with the police took the lives of my friends, Papa Jesus kept me safe and sound!

Born Thanksgiving night 1962, My Lord and Savior has allowed me, as a Black man in America, to survive The 1960's, The 1970's, The 1980's, The 1990's and the first 21 years of The New Millennium, **And Live To Tell About It!** Please do not think that I am bragging on myself by any stretch of the imagination, however, I am proudly boasting on what Jesus Christ has done for me in my lifetime! That is why I praise His Holy Name because I know exactly what He has done for me, over and over again. When I was in multiple situations where my ticket could have easily been punched, **He said, "No, Not Him!"**

Because of this, I have an attitude of gratitude. I know what God has done for me and I know exactly where I would have ended up if not for **The Mercy & Grace of God!** He is my Savior, my Creator, my Sustainer, my Redeemer and my Protector. He and He alone has thwarted Satan's attempts to derail my life and disrupt my relationship with The Lord. He has always shielded me from relentless Satanic bombardment. Jesus has always come to my aid and has been there to defeat Satan at every turn. No matter who I was with and no matter where I was, Jesus has always been there for me and I am thankful and grateful for His love, grace, mercy, benevolence and protection. If you have witnessed what He has done for you, then you can't help but acknowledge Him and develop an attitude of gratitude!

I know that you are in a very unsafe environment. I know that you can find evil within your environment faster than you can find good.

The things that you witness on the main yard, in the showers or in the dining facility are a testament to God's protection to His own. I know that things are not easy for you in this environment, but, I implore you to give your life, faith, hope and trust to Papa Jesus. He is our Creator, Sustainer, Redeemer and Protector. He and He alone will protect and support you the way that no one else can. I am a witness to this and I can personally guarantee that your life is better off with Him than without Him!

Having been a prisoner Himself, Our Lord and Savior has first hand knowledge of the penal system and all of its flaws. He knows what it is like to be stripped of your freedom, stripped of your dignity and surrounded by those who wish and seek to do you bodily harm. He knows what it's like to have a death sentence and understands execution all too well. Jesus knows, Jesus cares and most importantly, **Jesus Saves!** Jesus Christ is the answer to the human condition. He is the gateway to eternal happiness, the gatekeeper of the Kingdom Of Heaven and the architect of salvation. I invite you to ask Him for guidance and protection in your unsafe environment. Ask Him to send His angels to protect you from those who seek to surround you with evil. He is known for making a way when there is no way. He can take an impossible situation and miraculously make things possible. He is a can-do God in a world filled with potholes, snares, traps, pitfalls, dead-ends and no foreseeable way out!

He and He alone, can be victorious in a no-win scenario. He is joy to the joyless and hope to the hopeless. He is the master of miracles and He is the life-line to the lost. He cannot be defeated and He is anxiously awaiting your personal cry for help. He is knocking at the door to your heart and sincerely wants you to open that door to Him. Ask Him to come into your life and change your life for the better. Ask Him to adjust your current attitude and transform it into an attitude of gratitude. When He is your personal Lord and Savior, you will see a change in your life. Give your life to Him and watch the miracles happen. Please use this time in your life to make Him the centerpiece of your existence. The rewards are everlasting! God bless you my friend!

Sincerely,
Brother Griff

CHAPTER FOURTEEN

---~---

The Ultimate Ultimatum

November 15, 2021

Dear Friend,

I wish you nothing but peace, happiness and serenity on this new day that The Lord has made! We have made it to the eleventh month of this year and it is safe to say that 2021 is quickly coming to a close. The Lord Jesus Christ has delivered us to this new point in time and nothing but His grace, mercy and benevolence has shielded us from the onslaught of evil engulfing our world. Our God is a kind, merciful and loving God. His patience and forgiveness for His children is nothing short of miraculous!

Time, however, is not on our side when it comes to repentance. For those who are living contrary to God's wishes, there is a finite amount of time available to those who refuse to comply with God's law. Hebrews chapter 9 verse 27 says this:

"As it is appointed unto men once to die, but after this the judgment."

Those who live their lives according to the way of The Lord shall escape judgment through **The Plan Of Salvation**. Papa Jesus will reward those who acknowledge Him as Lord and Savior and He will judge those who reject Him as Savior and Lord Of All. Ezekiel chapter 18 verses 30 through 32 simply states:

30. Therefore I will judge you, O house of Israel, everyone according to his ways, saith The Lord God. Repent, and turn yourselves from all your transgressions; so iniquity shall not be your ruin.

31. Cast away from you all your transgressions, whereby ye have transgressed; and make you a new heart and a new spirit: for why will ye die, O house of Israel?

32. For I have no pleasure in the death of him that dieth, saith The Lord God: wherefore turn yourselves and live ye.

As children of God, we have been created first and foremost to serve God. The way that we present ourselves and interact with others should be a blatant testimony and glorification of God living within us. Nothing that we can do on our own is enough to warrant entry into God's Eternal Kingdom. We have all fallen short of the standard of excellence that He has set for us. Papa Jesus therefore came to Earth to sacrifice His life in order to pay the debt owed to God The Father for the sin of disobedience by Adam & Eve. He is The Lamb Of God, the Great and Almighty sacrifice, so that sins would be forgiven and modern man would have a second chance to live eternally and harmoniously with God The Father. Through His sacrifice, The Plan

Of Salvation was activated. Hebrews chapter 9 verse 28 states:

"So Christ was once offered to bear the sins of many; and unto them that look for him shall he appear the second time without sin unto salvation."

That, in and of itself, is cause for celebration. Jesus Christ has made salvation available to all who wish to live with God and abide by His laws. With this being the month of November, the Thanksgiving holiday is now upon us. Knowing that Our Lord and Savior Jesus Christ has paved the way for an eternal relationship with Him through The Plan Of Salvation is reason for Thanksgiving. He gave His life so that we may gain eternal life. He gave up glory and wrapped Himself in flesh in order to be sacrificed for us so that we can accept Him and achieve glory. The only thing that is required of us is to repent of our sins and ask Him to be Our Lord and Savior. Once that is done, get baptized in His name. That's all that it takes. You don't have to jump through hoops or jump over hurdles to achieve salvation. Just ask Papa Jesus to come into your heart, turn from darkness and walk toward the light. He is the way, the truth and the life. No man cometh unto The Father but by Him. He is The Gatekeeper of The Kingdom Of Heaven. He and He alone decides who gets in and who doesn't!

The question therefore is simple, will you accept Jesus Christ as your personal Lord and Savior? Will you reject Satan and all of his empty promises and make Jesus Christ your everything? I personally have given my life to Papa Jesus and He has delivered me from disastrous situations numerous times. Not only has He watched over me but He has watched out for me. He has made sure that me and my family have been protected by The Holy Spirit as we travel through this life. He has showered us with blessings over and over again. He has provided for us and sustained us constantly. Our lives are in His competent hands and even though things are not always perfect, we are safe and sound. God always has and always will, look out for his own.

The next question is; what do you prefer, salvation or condemnation? Do you prefer to choose Jesus Christ and gain eternal life? A life free of pain, misery and torment. Or do you prefer to reject Jesus Christ and allow yourself to be a part of The Great White Throne Judgment? A judgment scenario where no one is ever found innocent and all are sentenced to eternal damnation. Salvation or judgment? Judgment or salvation? It seems as though it would be a no-brainer doesn't it? Judgment equals death and salvation equals life. This is the ultimate ultimatum that man is faced with. Choose Papa Jesus or Satan. Choose life or death. Choose salvation or damnation. Don't let pride lead you to a bad end and please don't let what you **think** you know, become the catalyst for poor decision making!

Throughout my life, God has been there for me when nobody else was. I have personally witnessed His grace and mercy in action. I have tried to let others know what he has done for me and I have seen how some are anxious to learn more about The Lord whereas others just simply reject the notion that God exists at all. I have also been shocked to see how much evidence I can give a person that proves that God is alive and real and still they refuse to accept the fact that **He lives!** I have used the expression, **stuck on stupid,** many times, however, in this particular instance, the expression holds true! Please don't let this be your testimony!

The ultimate ultimatum, is something we all must face. **Either** and **or,** is something we all will answer willfully by choice or willfully by choosing not to choose. Nothing else will determine your eternal place of residence other than the decision you make with the ultimate ultimatum. **Either** you choose Jesus and life **or** you choose Satan and death. Papa Jesus is anxiously awaiting for you to make the right choice and let Him into your heart. Of all the choices that you will make within your lifetime, this is the most important. Of all the decisions that you will make within your lifetime, this will be the most relevant. Belief or disbelief, creation or evolution, religion or science, fact or fiction. The choice is yours to make and we all have a finite amount of time to make that decision. Jesus will allow you to make that choice and if you choose Him, He'll never let you down!

He will be there for you just like He has always been there for me. He was there for me when my siblings let me down and when my so called friends showed their true colors. He was there when my enemies had me outnumbered and when my friends could not be found. He has supported me, blessed me, chastised me, embraced me, shielded me, protected me and sustained me. He and He alone has brought me to this point in time and allowed me to prosper in His Holy Name. Papa Jesus is the foundation on which my life is built and my family and I will trust in Him until He calls us home. I want you to be victorious with the ultimate ultimatum and not another negative statistic in this the most important of all decisive scenarios. Please think about this and ask Him into your heart! God Bless You!

Sincerely,

Brother Griff

CHAPTER FIFTEEN

We All

December 7th, 2021

Dear Friend,

In the name of our Lord and Savior Jesus Christ I wish to greet you. Only through the grace of God have we made it to this the last month of the year 2021. So many things have happened in this year which lets you know how swiftly time is going by. In January we watched a riot take place at The U.S. Capital in an attempt to overturn the results of The 2020 Presidential Election. Shortly thereafter, we watched Ex-President Donald J.

Trump leave The White House and newly elected President Joseph R. Biden enter The White House.

We have witnessed the vaccines for Covid-19 become available for all age groups, in addition to, a Covid pill being produced to aid in the fight against the virus. Meanwhile, the death count continues to rise and hospitalization rates increase and overwhelm Intensive Care Units at an unprecedented rate. Hospitals are working with exhausted staff members who are coming down with Covid themselves. This pandemic has claimed the lives of millions of people all across the world with no foreseeable end in sight. This virus is continuously mutating into new variants which attack individuals no matter what their vaccination status is. As soon as we can give the "All Clear" from one version of the virus, another variant arises almost immediately. We also have been introduced to the Omicron variant of Covid-19, which originated in South Africa, and promises to become the dominant strain of this global virus replacing the Delta variant. Mandated mask wearing has now come back in many states, and in some cities, proof of vaccination status is now required to enter restaurants!

Just think, 80 years ago today, the Japanese attacked Pearl Harbor. An act which thrust The United States Of America into the second world war. This year we've witnessed The United States pull all troops out of Afghanistan, thereby ending the longest military engagement in American history. It seems as though the history of mankind is an endless cycle of warfare. If we're not fighting each other, we're fighting off Satan and his emissaries. No matter who or what we are battling, our God is still in control. Through His control, He walks with each and every one of us!

Since we are now in the last month of the year 2021 and with this being the last letter that I will write in this calendar year. I would like to share a poem with you that completely exemplifies God's walk with us. I do not know the name of the author but I do know the title. The poem is entitled, "Footprints In The Sand" and I hope that you will enjoy it!

Footprints In The Sand

One night I dreamed a dream.
As I was walking along the beach with my Lord.
Across the dark sky flashed scenes from my life.
For each scene, I noticed 2 sets of footprints in the sand.

One belonging to me and one to my Lord.
After the last scene of my life flashed before me,
I looked back at the last set of footprints in the sand.
I noticed that at many times along the path of my life,
Especially at the very lowest and saddest times,
There was only one set of footprints.
This really troubled me, so I asked The Lord about it.

"Lord, you said once I decided to follow you,
You'd walk with me all the way.
But I noticed that during the saddest
And most troublesome times of my life,
There was only one set of footprints.
I don't understand why, when I needed
You the most, You would leave me."

He whispered, "My precious child,
I love you and will never leave you,
Never, ever, during your trials and testings.
When you saw only one set of footprints,
It was then that I carried you."

This poem, in my opinion, is the embodiment of our walk with Papa Jesus through this life. **We all** have a personal Lord and Savior. His name is Jesus Christ. **We all** have a life-long opportunity to accept Him as our Lord and Savior and reap the benefits of His loving grace and mercy in our lives. **We all** have fallen short of the standard of excellence that He has set for our Earthly behavior. Knowing that, He created The Plan Of Salvation so that whosoever believes in Him shall be saved. **We all** have the opportunity to make Heaven our home for eternity and **we all** are works in progress. Jesus knocks at the door of each and every one of our hearts. He walks alongside us as we go throughout this life and He carries us when we can't make it on our own. **We all** have times in our lives when His help is the only help available to us. Therefore, **we all** must make the decision to either open the door to our hearts and let Him in, or, suffer the eternal consequences. Papa Jesus loves us more than we will ever know. **We all** have a golden opportunity to enjoy an eternal paradise with Him, if, we just open up our hearts and give our lives to Him!

 We all are suffering from a terminal case of mortality. None of us knows the time or place of our Earthly demise but we are all headed for it at breakneck speed. Some of us have decades left in our lives and others have just a few more minutes. Some of us have more birthdays behind us than we have ahead of us. Due to the failure of Adam & Eve to obey God's law, **we all** are living with the consequences of that failure. **We all** have a finite number of days given to each and every one of us. Remember how when we were kids, it seemed as if it took Christmas 5 years to get here? Now, as an adult, it seems like as soon as you pay off Christmas of last year on your credit cards, here it is again! I remember being told that I was too young to do certain things. Then, all of a sudden, I was in my prime. Now, I can plainly see that I'm looking back at the hands of time. Our days my friend, go by, oh, so quickly!

We all need The Lord and **we all** are running out of time. I humbly beseech you to give your life to Him. He is our Savior, our Creator and our Redeemer. He is the best friend that **we all** will ever have and the only friend that really and truly matters. Out of all the people that you try to impress, His opinion, is the only one that matters. He will never leave you, never abandon you and never let you down. Can you personally say that about your friends, about your family or about your associates? **We all** will stand in front of Him someday. Whether at The Judgment Seat Of Christ or at The Great White Throne Judgment, **we all** will face Him one way or the other. Do you want the outcome of that interaction to be glorious or terribly tragic? **We all** have the choice to make. **May Almighty God Walk With You As You Make Yours! Thank You For Your Time And God Bless You!**

Sincerely,
Brother Griff

My Plea To The Reader

———— ∾ ————

My friend, I seriously wish to thank you for taking the time to read this book. As you look around at this world that we are living in, I'd like for you to ponder this one simple question. Are things in your opinion getting better or are things getting worse? Take the time to give that question some serious thought. If you have ever read The Book Of Revelation, you will see exactly what God revealed to Saint John The Divine regarding the last days of time. If you know anything about building a puzzle, you always build the outside edges first, then you fill in the rest of the picture in the middle. As you watch news broadcasts or read a newspaper, you can see the edges of the puzzle of the last days of time being strategically placed into position. One by one, the framework of the end of days is being constructed right before our very eyes. Soon and very soon, the picture within the framework will begin to materialize. The Book Of Revelation is a play by play illustration of how this world will end and exactly what events will proceed the second coming of our Lord & Savior Jesus Christ! I suggest that you read it, so that you too will gain Revelation Knowledge!

In my opinion, things are definitely getting worse. War, crime, poverty, chaos and death aren't new concepts, however, the scale of how things have deteriorated, is truly mind boggling. Gun violence, whether at schools, houses of worship, shopping centers, workplaces or restaurants, has reached unprecedented levels. Incidents of road rage are being recorded now more than ever. Antisemitism is growing at record levels worldwide and trust in our government has plummeted dramatically. Drive-by shootings have become a common occurrence and the truth has become harder and harder to find, due to deception and conspiracy theories. It is also very plain to see, that division can be be seen everywhere you look. Whether you are referring to workplace cohesiveness, race, religion, sports, ethnicity, response to the Covid-19 pandemic or politics, people just seem unable or unwilling to agree on anything! In The 1990's, Rodney King asked a question that epitomizes the state of humanity. The question was; **"Can't we all just get along?"** Unity, can only be seen when it comes to The Six D's. Not The 1960's, but, The Six D's. The Six D's consist of deceit, disorganization, discontent, disharmony, dysfunction and discord. Common sense has become a very rare commodity and racial tensions have skyrocketed in the United States and abroad like never before!

Due to the growing number of police involved shootings and mistreatment of Black motorists and Blacks in general, calls for defunding police departments have been made nationwide. Scandals are par for the course in every walk of life, and, due to the acceptance of political correctness, we have witnessed the emergence of, The Cancel Culture. A culture in which a person is held accountable for anything said or done, years if not decades ago, and thereby ostracized in the future for it. A culture that seeks to discredit, disavow and destroy a person economically, politically and socially thereby making it next to impossible for them to maintain and retain their livelihood. A culture that mandates that a person lives a sinless, untarnished and unblemished life if you are to be a part of accepted society. Any deviation from established public norms is therefore cause for a witch-hunt into a persons past, resulting in a barrage of negative publicity, with the intent of ruining the future of the individual in question! This is utterly ridiculous because, the last time I checked, we are all sinners, and, the only person who ever lived a flawless and perfect life was our Lord & Savior Jesus Christ!

It appears as though people have never heard the story of Jesus being confronted by the high ranking Jews of His era, Scribes & Pharisees, who tried to trap Jesus by bringing a woman, caught in the act of adultery, before Him. They claimed that the Mosaic Law clearly dictated that the woman should be stoned to death. They brought her before Him and asked Him what fate should befall her. Jesus knew that this was just a transparent ploy, another feeble attempt, to try to legally trap and ensnare Him. Jesus hit them with a One-Liner that literally stopped them in their tracks. Jesus looked at them and said, **"Let he who is without sin, cast the first stone."** One by one, her accusers left, knowing very well that they weren't sinless, until the only people left were Jesus, His disciples and the woman. Jesus asked her, **"Woman, where are those thine accusers? Hath no man condemned thee?"** She replied, "No man Lord." Jesus therefore told her, **"Neither do I condemn thee: Go, and sin no more!"**

This simple story emphasizes how even though over 2000 years have gone by since that occurred, man really hasn't changed at all. The Holy Bible reveals to us that, **"There is nothing new under the sun!"** A statement which still holds true to this day. People sin today just like they sinned during the times when Jesus walked this Earth. Sin has just become so widespread, that now it is just another common occurrence in our daily lives. Sin has not changed, however, the technology used to commit sin, has definitely changed. I would also like to remind those who are active participants of The Cancel Culture, of this one sobering fact. When referring to mankind, Jesus also stated that: **<u>"None are righteous, no, not one!"</u>**

My friend, my plea to you is for you to read the word of God and develop a relationship with Him. We are closer to the end of days now more than ever. Only God The Father knows exactly when the end will come, but, it is safe to say that we are closer to it now than we were yesterday. The stage is being set for the second coming of The Lord and the signs are plain to see. I plea and beseech you to accept Papa Jesus before it is too late. The writing is on the wall, the evidence is all around, and, before you know it, it will be too late! Please ask Papa Jesus to forgive you of your sins, get baptized in His Holy Name and live your life according to God's law. Life is too short and it is my utmost desire for you to be prepared for His arrival. **We all will stand in His presence some day!** I want you to be one of those who will be gladly accepted into His Kingdom, because you gave your life to Him. **He will present you faultless before the presence of His glory with exceeding joy!**

Gil Burnett Griffin

2022

ACKNOWLEDGMENTS

$\approx$

I would like to thank my personal Lord & Savior Jesus Christ for using me as His vessel to get His word to those who have lost their freedom. After completing the first book, Pastor James Moore Jr. challenged me to create a follow up sequel. Not being one who wants to let down a dear friend, I took him up on this challenge. Hopefully, this second book, will continue to drive home some of the thoughts and ideas discussed in the prequel, in addition to, sharing new insights on our faith. I am just grateful for this opportunity to share my observations with those who could benefit from them. It is my intention that this book, although written to the incarcerated, be used by many various out-reach programs around the world to introduce Christianity to those who do not know The Lord!

Antoinette "Shaun" Miles, the director of our Prison Outreach Ministry, has worked tire-lessly with me. She has been highly instrumen-tal in leading me to the directors of some of San Diego's leading drug and homeless outreach pro-grams. I am hoping that in the future, this book could be used to help all sorts of people develop a sincere relationship with The Lord no mat-ter what they are going through. Whether you are dealing with drug dependency, alcoholism, homelessness, foster care, abusive relationships, suicide prevention, gang outreach, incarceration or just desiring to get more information regard-ing Our Lord & Savior Jesus Christ. This book can be used for many different types of outreach programs worldwide. I wish to invite all who want to get to know The Lord better, to give this book a good read. It is a spiritual supplement to The Holy Bible, created to foster and inspire greater biblical knowledge and appreciation. We all need more inspiration and hope in our lives. Thank you so much Shaun & Pastor James Moore Jr. for all or your assistance in getting this book into the hands of outreach program directors. So many people are lost and in need of all types of assistance, in addition to, spiritual guidance. I am forever grateful for your leadership, understanding, encouragement, enthusiasm and endless optimism. Your support will never be forgotten and you truly are a blessing to our Prison Ministry!

Deacon Michael Foreman and Brother Steve Synder have both been very valuable sources of inspiration and encouragement throughout this process. Each of us have lost someone very dear to us within the past year. Deacon Foreman lost his beautiful bride of 13 years, Brother Steve lost his mother and I lost my brother Calvin who was the best big brother that a kid could ever ask for. Aside from my father, Paul Griffin Jr., I've never been that close to any other family member ever. Fortunately, all of the loved ones that the three of us lost, knew The Lord and we all rest assuredly knowing that they all are with Our Heavenly Father In Paradise! Deacon Foreman and Brother Steve have not only befriended and inspired me unselfishly, also, we have developed a unique Christian brotherhood. A kindred fellowship which is greatly and sincerely appreciated. My life has definitely benefited from listening to their diverse perspectives and valuable viewpoints. They have encouraged me and have completely enhanced my outlook emphatically. I thank God Almighty for placing them in my life at just the right time. The Good Lord always places an angel, or two, in your path precisely when you need them! Mere words cannot express the amount of love that I have for both of these gentlemen who have become more than just friends to me. **They truly are my brothers in Christ, Thank You, from the bottom of my heart!**

I have been blessed with a wonderful set of In-laws. They currently live in the Philippines, and with God's help, we plan to bring them to America to live with us. Rudolfo & Leticia Mallari, affectionately known as Lolo & Lola, are the most supportive and compassionate In-laws that I could ever ask for. Their Lovely daughter, Lerma Catap Mallari Griffin, is the love of my life. After 14 years of marriage, our love has grown stronger with each passing day.

She has given birth to the biggest blessing that Papa Jesus ever bestowed to either one of us aside from our salvation. That blessing is our beautiful daughter Delenn Mallari Griffin. Lerma and Delenn have enhanced my life immeasurably and I thank Papa Jesus multiple times a day for placing each one of them in my life. My wife, my daughter and my In-laws, have loved, encouraged, inspired, helped and cheered me on like no other set of individuals ever have. I know with all my heart that with Jesus Christ as Our Lord & Savior, **The Best Is Yet To Come! Thanks For Reading, Thanks For Your Support And God Bless You!**

ABOUT THE AUTHOR

Gil Burnett Griffin is a member of The New Paradise Baptist Church Prison Outreach Ministry. He and the pastor of NPBC, Reverend James Moore Jr., have known each other since they were three years old and met in the Sunday School Nursery Department of Calvary Baptist Church in San Diego, California. Baptized at age six/seven by the late Dr. S.M. Lockridge, Gil was a member of the CBC Sunday School Program until his departure to The University Of California San Diego in 1983. There he was a member of the

Warren College Residence Halls Staff of Resident Advisors from 1984 until shortly before his graduation in 1986.

Primarily a graduate of San Diego City College in 1983, Gil has an AA Degree in Business and a BA Degree in Media Productions. Married in 2008 at NPBC he and his wife Lerma and their daughter Delenn officially joined the church in August of 2017. Officially retired July of 2019, Gil has now returned to his passion for writing in the hopes of pursuing this as a retirement career. "<u>Sincerely, Brother Griff Volume 2</u>" is his second book of inspiration and hope aimed at helping the incarcerated find their way to Christ. His daughter Delenn is an aspiring artist and they hope to work on various projects together in the near future!